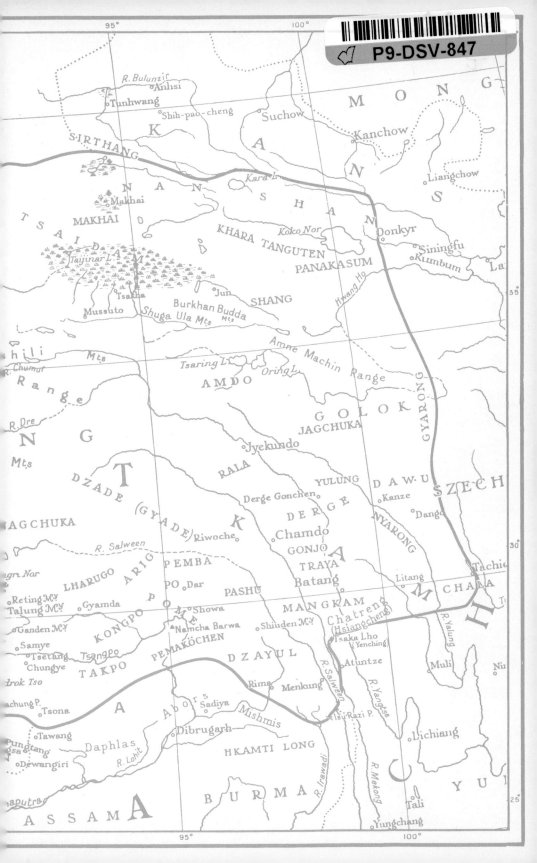

95°   100°

R. Bulunzir
        Anhsi
    Tunhwang
        Shih-pao-cheng   Suchow
                                            Kanchow
K A N S U
S·IRTHANG   Liangchow
                    Kara L.
N A N   S H A N
    Makhai   Koko Nor   Donkyr
MAKHAI   KHARA TANGUTEN   Siningfu
                PANAKASUM   Kumbum   La
TSAIDAM
    Taijinar L.   SHANG   Hwang Ho   35
    Tsacha   Jun
Mussuto   Burkhan Budda Mts
        Shuga Ula Mts
hili   Mts
R. Chumur   Tsaring L.   Oring L.   Amne Machin Range
R a n g e   AMDO
R. Dre   G O L O K
N   G   JAGCHUKA
Mts   RALA   Jyekundo
                                    YULUNG   D A W U   S Z E C H
    DZADE (GYADE)   Derge Gonchen   Kanze   Dango
                K   DERGE   NYARONG
    Riwoche   Chamdo   Tachie
R. Salween   GONJO
GAGCHUKA   ARIG   PEMBA   TRAYA   Litang   CHALA
egri Nor   LHARUGO   PO Dar   PASHU   Batang   M
Reting M.Y   Gyamda   Showa   MANGKAM   R. Yalung
Talung M.Y   Shiuden M.Y   Chatreng
Ganden M.Y   KONGPO   Namcha Barwa   (Hsiangcheng)   H
Samye   PEMAKOCHEN   Tsaka Lho   Muli   Nin
Tsetang   Tsangpo   DZAYUL   (Yenching)
Chungye   TAKPO   Atuntze
rok Tso   Abors   Sadiya   Rima   Menkong
achung P.   A   Mishmis   R. Salween   Lichiang
Tsona   Tawang   Tsu-Razi P.   R. Yangtse   C   Y U
Pundtang   Dibrugarh   R. Lohit
gsa   Dewangiri   Daphlas   HKAMTI LONG   R. Mekong   Tali
aputra   Yungchang
A S S A M A   B U R M A

95°   100°

TIBET: HEART OF ASIA

THE WHEEL OF LIFE

Picturing the Buddhist Theory of the Universe.

TIBET

Heart of Asia

LAURA PILARSKI

THE BOBBS-MERRILL COMPANY, INC.

INDIANAPOLIS   NEW YORK

Text copyright © 1974 by Laura Pilarski
Illustrations copyright © 1974 by the Bobbs-Merrill Company, Inc.

Published by the Bobbs-Merrill Company, Inc.
Indianapolis   New York

ISBN 0-672-51594-6
Library of Congress catalog card number: 73-13232

Designed by Jack Jaget

Manufactured in the United States of America

First printing

To Tibetan refugees everywhere,
with special regard
for those whom
I have met and come to
know in Switzerland

Contents

INTRODUCTION 1

CHAPTER 1. *The Earthly Realm* 5

CHAPTER 2. *Early Kings, Legendary and Real* 14

CHAPTER 3. *Legacy of a Hundred Thousand Songs* 23

CHAPTER 4. *Tibet and the Mongol Rulers* 29

CHAPTER 5. *The Rise of God-Kings* 35

CHAPTER 6. *The Great Fifth and Merry Sixth* 43

CHAPTER 7. *Under the Manchus* 50

CHAPTER 8. *Lhasa: "God's Place"* 57

CHAPTER 9. *The Making of a Monk* 64

CHAPTER 10. *Tibetan Ways of Life* 73

CHAPTER 11. *Rites, Mysticism and Magic* 83

CHAPTER 12. *Independence Under the Thirteenth* 89

CHAPTER 13. *The End of Freedom* 94

CHAPTER 14. *Invasion and the Aftermath* 101

CHAPTER 15. *The God-King Chooses Exile* 110

BIBLIOGRAPHY 118

INDEX 121

LIST OF ILLUSTRATIONS

WHEEL OF LIFE ii

LHASA TEMPLE 59

POTALA 60

TRUMPETS ANNOUNCE THE DAWN 62

A LAMASERY 65

TIBETAN WIND-HORSE 68

ABBOT OF A MONASTERY 69

TIBETAN PRAYER WHEEL 70

TIBETAN PRAYER CYLINDER 71

LAMA IN DEMON COSTUME 84

TIBET: HEART OF ASIA

Introduction

THERE is no strict transliteration of Tibetan into English. Different systems exist to romanize the words, and this has led to a range of English spellings. The patron deity of the country, for example, appears in authoritative sources as "Chenrezi," "Chenrezig," "Chenresi," "Chenresig" and "Chenrazee." In this compilation the more commonly used English spellings have been chosen.

Also, it must be pointed out that hard facts of history are elusive in Tibetan annals, with not much agreement on what are generally considered basic matters, at least in the western way of thinking. Leading chroniclers tend to conflict with one another, even in such fundamental areas as chronology, and lack any critical perspective. The records of the times were written primarily by lamas, who understandably concentrated more on the supernatural than on any natural description of events.

Probably Sir Charles Bell, the English diplomat, scholar and author of definitive works on Tibet, most accurately characterized the Tibetan sense of history when he declared: "History, unless it centers on religion, does not appeal to the Tibetan mind."

Stretched into the shape of a heart in central Asia lies a legendary land, a land of many titles and many myths. This is Tibet, "The Hermit Kingdom," "The Land of Snows," "The Roof of the World," "The Forbidden Land," "Land of a Thousand Buddhas." Lifted well above the customary dwelling levels on earth, this uncommon realm remained hidden from the trafficking outside world—particularly the western world—for most of its history. In Tibet, history emerged not so much the story of a people as a chronicle of religion. The rhythms of life stemmed from the special Tibetan cult of Buddhism, tied in with exotic customs quite different from those of powerful neighboring countries like China and India. Not without some difficulty, the Tibetans had come to shape their own destiny, or believed they had. . . .

To the western mind Tibet represented an improbable kingdom. A country ruled by a god-king, a ruler not hereditary, not elected, not chosen by peers to his office, but very directly "discovered"? Impossible! A country where residents incessantly whirled prayer wheels to invoke the gods and respected the wheel in religious symbolism, yet never used the wheel as a form of transportation? Incredible! A country where citizens liked to travel about on pilgrimages, visits and trading expeditions, but where—because people were expected to give hospitality to anyone who asked for it—no hotels, no restaurants, no tearooms existed? Unthinkable! A country seen from the outside as "medieval" and "feudal" in its social system, but whose inhabitants are described by objective observers as sunny, serene and satisfied? Inconceivable!

Comprehensible or not, these were some of the facts of life in the cloud-hidden kingdom preserved from prying eyes by geography and by a policy of self-imposed isolation. Only the most hardy and determined of visitors succeeded in piercing the natural barriers of the country. Along the extensive southern border the Himalayas, the world's loftiest mountains, stood sentinel; once past this hurdle, the traveler faced turbulent rivers, secluded valleys, treeless plains, terrifying winds, and the vast, uninhabited spaces of the highlands. Over the centuries those pioneers who managed to conquer the barriers could easily be counted. These were missionaries, merchants, explorers, adventurers, scholars, diplomats and writers, and their reports commanded fascinated attention.

In the United States, former commentator Lowell Thomas and his author-son, Lowell Thomas, Jr., probably did the most to popularize the exotic story and presence of Tibet. Americans too were captivated by the image of Shangri-La conjured by the English novelist James Hilton in *Lost Horizon*, the story of an imaginary eternal haven of incredible happenings which could be credible in only one country of the world: Tibet.

No doubt the popular modern view of the remote Asian land tends to be more romantic than sober, more magical than realistic, with Tibet visualized as unchanging, everlasting and indestructible. Yet even the most practical-minded of visitors to Tibet have come away imbued with the idyllic appeal of the land, culture and people. Consider, for example, the sentimental farewell of the first British native to cross the Tibetan frontier on a mission of commercial reconnaissance: "Farewell, ye honest and simple people," wrote the hard-headed George Bogle in 1775. "May ye long enjoy that happiness which is denied to more polished nations; and while they are engaged in the endless pursuit of avarice and ambition, defended by your barren mountains, may ye continue to live in peace and contentment, and know no wants but those of nature."

Certainly, so far as any nation was able to do so, Tibet lived apart and alone. The people took some comfort from their own proverb which assured them: "If the valley is reached by a high pass, only the best friends or worst enemies are visitors." Through the different periods of history, not many enemies have trod on their soil. Even the wide-ranging Mongol invasions of the thirteenth century touched Tibet only in the northeast and in some of the eastern districts; the invaders ventured no farther. This despite the fact that the Mongols were "neighbors" and overran a vast portion of Asia and Europe. And that indefatigable early traveler Marco Polo never did enter Tibet, though he explored Asiatic lands far and near. In different centuries, conflicts arose between Tibet and its bordering lands. During the Manchu protectorate, Chinese military expeditions were dispatched to Tibet. But Tibet never became part of Chinese territory. Tibetans saw their own insularity as a national condition to be recognized and respected by other nations.

Small wonder then that when, in October 1950, the fateful announcement was flashed that Communist Chinese troops had stormed over the borders of Tibet, the news was received with disbelief. Nations of the world seemed unwilling or unprepared to accept this invasion. Even the Tibetans, who had been forewarned that they were to be "liberated," clung to the hope of prayers and new negotiations to reverse their situation. Before that moment of invasion, there had been at best an uneasy truce between Tibet and China; their record of complicated political relations stretched back some thirteen centuries.

Recent history had cast Tibet in the role of a buffer state amidst the giant Asian powers, but now it had been seized as a strategic prize. The People's Republic of China, seeking to solidify its borders and its power on the Asian continent, saw the country as a natural fort in the heart of Asia and as a future bastion for Chinese airpower. The clash of arms was brief—the Tibetans had no war machine to withstand such an invasion—and Tibet, once proud and spiritually autonomous, became "annexed" as a region of China. But this was not yet the end of historic Tibet. In 1959 the land, its people and their god-king figured in dramatic events that made headlines around the world. But all developments pointed to an undeniable conclusion: The curtain had been forcibly drawn on a unique civilization.

CHAPTER ONE

The Earthly Realm

THE LAND and people of Tibet have been variously described, but not in more impertinent words than those of a titled Englishman who dismissed the country as "a huge monastery inhabited by a nation of monks, with a subject population inhabiting the most inhospitable region in the world, in the worst climate which is habitable by human beings." Only as an exaggeration is this statement notable.

To begin with, and contrary to a widely held notion, Tibet is not all snow and rugged mountains. Most of the area is a vast tableland called Chang Tang (Northern Plain) stretching some 1,500 miles from east to west at an average altitude of 15,000 feet. This elevated plateau is virtually cut off from neighboring territories by the world's highest mountain ranges. These mountains represent the eternal "Abode of Snows."

Along the southern border sweep the majestic Himalayas, with the landmark Mt. Everest towering at 29,028 feet. To the west there is the Ladakh range, with the Karakoram, an extensive complex, farther to the north. The Kunlun range, reputed to be one of the oldest in the world, forms the northern flank of Tibet. To the east a network of almost impassable rivers have carved out deep gorges that are an equally formidable barrier to human traffic. Only to the northeast is there a gap in the protecting ramparts. This is the doorway that has been used by invaders.

The Chinese province of Sinkiang (Chinese Turkestan) borders Tibet on the north. On the east lie the Chinese provinces of Chinghai and Sikang, whose political boundaries with Tibet never have been clearly demarked. Tibet's neighbor on the west is Kashmir, where the Western Himalayas meet the Karakoram mountains. The Himalayan hill states of Nepal, Bhutan, Sikkim and India—in upper Assam—ring the southern boundary of Tibet.

Since Tibet is the highest country in the world, with settlements nestled even at 10,000 feet above sea level, with roads that cross 15,000-foot passes and mountains reaching to some 25,000 feet, it is often pictured as very cold, very wild, and most inhospitable. The country's latitude, however, is the latitude of Algeria. While the climate can be subzero, it also can be blazing hot during summer days. The annual rainfall is estimated at 15 inches, and sometimes no rain or snow falls for many months. The clear air is cold, but, as it is described by travelers, "dry as the air of the desert" and incredibly exhilarating. Wild and inhospitable stretches do exist, but they are broken up by fertile, gentle, pastoral places. The wide diversity of local climates and conditions within Tibet prompted an early Chinese traveler to coin the maxim: "Every ten *li* (a distance of about three miles), heaven is different." A more current proverb proclaims: "Each district has its own way of speaking."

Concerning area and population, a confusing array of calculations exists, depending on whether Tibet is seen as a geographic, an ethnic or a political unit. Contemporary western sources of information offer statistics on area ranging from 463,000 to 700,000 square miles. But 475,000 square miles seems a reasonably accurate figure. (Chinese sources usually list Tibet's area, including the disputed Chamdo district in the east, as 1,221,600 square kilometers.) "Ethnic" Tibet extends into the population of Bhutan, Sikkim, Nepal and several provinces of China; the total ranges from three to six million. There appears to be some consensus that "Tibet proper"—the political entity governed directly through the capital, Lhasa— consists of some 1,500,000 residents, with at least twice this number of "ethnic" Tibetans. No real census or complete survey of the land mass has ever been done—and both measurements have varied through the centuries—so it is not surprising that exact figures do not exist. So far as "political" Tibet is concerned, one must remember that it was not politics but religion that united the people.

Western research places the Tibetan people among the Mongolian tribes who came partly from the northeast and later from Assam, and from Burma in the southeastern part of Asia. But the origins of Tibetans still remain somewhat of a mystery. Anthropologists distinguish two main types: The short-statured Tibetan with high cheekbones and a flat nose, found primarily in the farmer population, and the taller, longer limbed Tibetan with almost aquiline features who generally lives the life of a herdsman. Scholars and travelers to the country have been struck by the prevalence in some areas of what they describe as a "Red Indian" type physically similar to the North American Indian. "European" type Tibetans with blue eyes and blond hair also have been observed, mostly in the northeast. Visitors who have spent longer periods in Tibet confirm that the average Tibetan is at once distinguishable from a Chinese and resembles even less his southern neighbors in India.

Tibetans themselves give a wondrously fanciful explanation of how the earth and their own land emerged and of their own beginnings. Their story of creation goes like this: There was darkness at the beginning; nothing more. A wind came, moving quietly and gently. From this wind a giant thunderbolt was formed in the shape of a cross. Then clouds appeared, and

an endless rain began to fall. Each drop of rain was big enough
to cause a flood, and when the rain finally subsided, it had
created Gyatso, the primeval ocean. Tibet lay under this ocean,
but in the course of a longer period and other legendary
events, the water dried up, leaving Tibet surrounded by great
mountains. At first it was a land of valleys and hills and juniper
forests inhabited only by invisible and intangible spirits. So
goes the legend.

Rather remarkably, geologists tend to support the basic
thesis of this Tibetan version of their physical world: They
confirm that the Tibetan tableland was once the bottom of a
vast sea, the Sea of Thetys.

Development of human life on this tableland, according to
Tibetan accounts, stemmed from the mating of a monkey and
a mountain ogress or she-demon. The monkey happened to
be the protégé of Chenrezi, the merciful patron deity of Tibet,
and had been sent to meditate in the Land of Snows. The
ogress appeared to him as a beautiful woman to lure him from
his contemplation, but no mere female charm could dissuade
the monkey from his destined task. One version of the tale
is that the she-demon then threatened to marry a demon and
breed generations of ogres and ogresses, and this caused the
concerned monkey to review the situation. Another relates
that the pitiful crying and loneliness of the ogress filled the
monkey with compassion. In any event, the monkey consulted
his patron god, and it came to pass that the monkey married
the ogress, who bore him six children.

These children, some interpretations explain, represented the
six varieties of creatures inhabiting the world: gods, demi-gods,
ghosts, human beings, animals and fiends. But the general
story of Tibetan genesis relates that these offspring became real
people, the first Tibetans, who lived and multiplied and began
to cultivate the soil, raising crops of barley and wheat. As
human beings, these early inhabitants inherited good traits like
fortitude, piety and charity from their monkey progenitor,

and less desirable traits like greed, lust and bad temper from their ogress progenitor.

Tibetans believe their human history began in the south of the country, in the valley of Yarlung south of the Tsangpo River. The place where the six original children grew up is now known as Tse-Tang ("playground") and is one of the principal towns in the area. The Yarlung district, one of the most fertile in Tibet, later in history became the cradle of royal power from which emerged the early kings who ruled the country. The story of their beginnings is told and retold among Tibetans, and children like to repeat it among themselves. Whimsical as the story may seem, it does bring to mind the accepted western Darwinian theory of man's development from the ape.

In the southlands stretch verdant pastures, river valleys, the "breadbasket" farming districts, villages and cities, the trade routes, woodlands and flower-studded meadows. Here the great Tsangpo, the country's economic artery, cuts across a course of more than 800 miles before eventually bending south into India, to reappear as the Brahmaputra. The Tsangpo is swelled by tributaries in the two central provinces of Tibet, and sometimes this lifeline valley, along with its side-valleys, reaches two-hundred-mile widths. Altitudes in this area generally range from 7,000 to 12,000 feet. Some of the farmland is irrigated by an ancient canal system. Rain tends to be sparse, but sunshine is plentiful, and crops such as barley, wheat, and buckwheat and an assortment of fruits and vegetables, including onions, tomatoes and peas, are cultivated. Basically, the economy rests on grain agriculture and animal husbandry.

This cultivated south contrasts dramatically with the north, where the Chang Tang covers more than half the face of Tibet, consisting of barren, rocky land dotted with salt lakes and some scrub vegetation. Powerful winds often sweep these heights, sometimes reaching hurricane fury, and, in the winter, temperatures dip to thirty and forty degrees below zero.

Through this wilderness, except in the extreme north, roam the hardy nomads with their herds of sheep, yak—similar to the American buffalo—and cattle. The yak, the most useful of all animals in Tibet, supplies milk, meat and hides as well as transportation. The plateau region, though an area of natural and physical hardship, offers endless spectacular vistas which travelers have described in rhapsodic terms as resembling a mirage in the desert. The cold, thin, diaphanous air seems to cast its own spell.

To the east, between Chang Tang and the frontier of China, the mountain ranges stretch from north to south rather than west to east. The mighty rivers of the Salween, Mekong and Yangtze flow through this eastern territory. Their upper, lower and middle reaches bear different Tibetan and Chinese names as they flow southward, cutting deep parallel gorges that present almost impassable barriers to travelers. The chief routes from China proper to central Tibet stay well to the northeast, where they cross the headstreams at higher elevations. In these eastern lands lie rich mineral deposits of gold, silver, copper, iron and lead. These have not been mined extensively, however, because Tibetans believe that disturbing the earth disturbs the gods as well.

The western part of the country is, overall, desolate and sparsely populated. Here, however, is a tremendous watershed area where the Tsangpo arises and two great rivers of India— the Indus and Sutlej—have their source. In the southwest, snow-peaked Mt. Kailas and the turquoise Lake Manasarowar were revered as holy places in Hindu as well as Buddhist cosmography, attracting pilgrims from a wide area. District trading centers flourished too.

The people of Tibet—tribes, really, in the beginning— showed an early appreciation for the quality, the beauty, and the extraordinary diversity of their land. In an ancient poem the country is acclaimed as "the center of high snow mountains, the source of great rivers, a lofty country, a pure land." Tibetans named their country *Bod* (pronounced Pö), which was variously rendered by Indian neighbors to the south as *Bhota, Bhauta* or *Bauta*. It is suggested that this is the name that can be found in a first-century Greek narrative where a people of central Asia called the Bautai are mentioned. The modern name of Tibet derives from designations given by near and far neighbors, from the Mongolian *Thubet*, the ancient Chinese *Tu-fan*, the Thai *Thibet*, and the Arabic *Tubbat*. Historic trade routes connected Tibet with her neighbors, usually to specific trading points in border areas. The remote land has never been a regularly traversed passage for migratory peoples or world-conquering armies.

Historically, it took many centuries for Tibet to become unified, and its administrative groupings have varied. Modern Tibet consisted of these principal regions: Ü and Tsang (central Tibet), Amdo and Kham (eastern Tibet), and Ngari (western Tibet). Among themselves, Tibetans say the best religion comes from the central region, the best fighters from Kham, and the best businessmen from Amdo.

Although territorially an expansive land, Tibet has cradled only a few large cities: The almost apocryphal Lhasa, the capital and the Vatican of Lamaism, which is the Tibetan version of Buddhism; Shigatse, an important administrative center; Gyantse, an economic center and the main wool market; and Chamdo, a regional headquarters located on a significant trade route leading eastward into China. All of these places are on general routes used for trade and travel, and except for Chamdo all are situated in central Tibet. From Lhasa ("God's Place") emanated civil government as well as spiritual power. The strength of government dwindled as it diffused into remoter areas of the country, but not the people's loyalty to it. It is estimated that Lhasa had political "control" of at most half of all Tibetan territory at a given time. While political parties were unknown, this did not preclude a variety of secular intrigues and rivalries among prominent families, nobles, monasteries, and lay and religious leaders. Such quarrels served to weaken the centralized governmental authority.

As a church-state, Tibet was ruled for centuries by the Dalai Lama or god-king. In theory, all land belonged to the state, with the nobility and the great monasteries holding vast portions. Realistically, probably thirty percent of landed property belonged to the state, forty percent to monasteries and the rest to aristocratic families. The entire structure of political and social life was bound up with the land system.

While the Dalai Lama exercised supreme power in both religious and secular affairs, his apparatus for overall governing was not so unsophisticated. He ruled with the help of a regent or prime minister and an executive body of laymen and monks called the *Kashag*, and he could call a national assembly into session when necessary. There were specific administrative national offices—for example, that of assessor of revenues—and district government was under the guidance of the *Dzong-pön*, another type of official. The country was divided into a hundred or so regions under district administration. District administrators and their adjutants collected taxes, dispensed justice and generally maintained law and order. It was at the district and village level that government touched the ordinary Tibetans, who were spread throughout the country, living mostly as farmers, herdsmen and traders. They did not have much to say about how they were governed, and throughout their history there is no record of a popular uprising against governmental control as such. But Tibetans did at times lodge complaints against rapacious officials on the village or district level.

To a degree, Tibet could be termed "a nation of monks." Thousands of monasteries dotted the land, and at least twenty percent of the entire male population lived and learned in them. The monastic life was open to all, rich or poor, scholars or illiterates; and the title of "lama" or priest-teacher was greatly honored. Monasteries were centers of education, and their idealistic goal was to serve the lay populace through prayer, religious services and teachings. They also served as libraries, art galleries, and training headquarters for craftsmen and artisans, all religiously oriented. The biggest monasteries housed some 20,000 monks and functioned as self-contained financial, administrative and academic units. The land and wealth they owned were staggering, and the power they could wield was equally astounding. Monks and monasteries put a unique stamp on Tibet, and without them the country would be almost impossible to explain.

For the average Tibetan, there is not much that does not begin and end with religion. Religion has molded the Tibetans' outlook on life (generally cheerful), fashioned their customs and traditions and character (rather strikingly original), and determined their social and political institutions. Had not the earthly realm been so isolated, the whole history of Tibet could have been altered. As it developed, however, an unearthly realm came to envelop the purely earthly one.

CHAPTER TWO

Early Kings,
Legendary and Real

TO SEPARATE fact from fiction in accounts purporting to trace the earliest centuries of Tibetan history is practically impossible. Standard chronologies tend to begin with the seventh century A.D., when Tibet emerged as an imperial power under its first historical king. Prior to this time, hard facts about early life in Tibet remain obscure. Scholars surmise that pastoral and nomadic people roamed the land in prehistoric times. Chiefly shepherds and yak herdsmen, these dwellers moved with the seasons, taking refuge in caves hollowed from the mountains but also living in tents. Authority rested in the family, with power over a clan or tribe passing from father to son. Strong clans and chieftains tended to take over weaker ones.

Early inhabitants are presumed to have been similar in appearance to present-day Tibetans, but they were warlike in behavior and had a distinct taste for banditry. The first land to be cultivated was in southeastern Tibet, where the soil supported both grazing and farming. From this more fertile and more settled area stemmed strong political power achieved through bigger groupings of tribes and eventually a line of kings. Prominent chieftains gave a visible sign of their growing importance by building fortified hill structures as a protection against rival tribes and against invading neighbors.

Tibetan sources describing the country's early history are more epic than exact, lingering on tradition and myth rather than on deeds and dates. But what they recount is delightfully curious, picturesquely drawn, and well worth retelling.

More or less uniformly, these chronicles list some twenty-seven legendary kings. This royal line originated in India, where the son of a noble family was born with long turquoise eyebrows, a full set of teeth, and webbed fingers. "Apprehending great evil from such ominous signs in the infant," according to one rendition of the tale, "the parents packed it up in a copper vessel and floated it away on the river Ganges." The infant was found by a farmer, who took it home and cared for it. In time the child grew up and wandered northward across the Himalayas into Tibet. There he met some herdsmen grazing their cattle. When the herdsmen asked him where he had come from, the young prince—who of course did not speak their language—gestured upward toward the sky and the mountains over which he had come. The Tibetans, who regarded the sky as sacred, concluded that he was very holy. Deciding to make him their leader, they lifted him onto their shoulders. They named him *Nyatri Tsenpo*—"He who was carried in victory upon the back."

There were seven in this first line of mythical kings, and their dynasty is distinguished by an absence of earthly burial places. They all had tombs in the sky, to which they ascended after death with the aid of what are described only as "sky-ropes." But the eighth king did leave a corpse and a tomb behind, so it is presumed he somehow cut the "sky-rope" that would have conducted him to heaven. One version is that he argued with one of his ministers, who as a result used magic against him and severed the "ladder" connecting earth and sky. The first rulers were grouped under different royal lines and were sometimes credited with very practical accomplishments

such as irrigation canals in valley basins, ordering a livestock
census for tax purposes, and introducing the plow.

Tibetan tradition places the first appearance of Buddhism in
the country during the reign of Lhato Thori (King Powerful
Delicate Tower), a ruler considered more mortal than legendary. One day while he was up on the roof of his palace, as
the story goes, a casket fell out of the sky and landed at his
feet. The mysteriously delivered gift contained books of
Buddhist canon, a model of a golden pagoda, and the six
sacred syllables (*Om mani padme hum*) that comprise the
Tibetan prayer of everlasting truth. Esoteric explanations of
the six-syllable prayer "*Om Mani Padme Hum*" abound, and
whole books have even been written about it. In translation,
the words mean: "Hail to the Jewel in the Lotus." Simply
explained, this invocation, addressed to Chenrezi, salutes the
"Jewel" (none other than the Buddha) in the "Lotus" (the
heart). Thus, the rendering emerges: "Hail to the Buddha in
our Hearts." Merely uttering these six syllables was believed to
stop the cycle of rebirth and transport the reciter directly to
paradise.

The king had no idea what these offerings represented, but
he wisely preserved them all and worshipped the books daily,
naming them "Hidden Greatness." Later, in a dream, he was
advised that the secret of the books would be revealed to a
future generation.

The real starting point of Tibetan history was about
A.D. 625, when Songtsen Gampo (Straight-Strong-Deep) assumed the throne to inaugurate a period of independence
under native kings and princes. Ordinarily he is designated as
the thirty-third king, so between the legendary twenty-seven
and the first historical leader must have come five other kings of
which there is no exact record. Songsten Gampo was exactly
what Tibet needed: a powerful and decisive monarch. Until the
seventh century, Tibetans had not figured as a people or as a
unified land; there were different clans headed by chieftains
vying for leadership and recognition. The kingdom of Tibet

grew and became consolidated through the centuries as individual chieftains acquired the support and allegiance of other clan leaders and emerged as dominant figures. When Songtsen Gampo came to power, Tibet was rather effectively unified and shaped. Like other Asian lands of this period, it was a warring nation. Through battle, the king extended the military and political influence of Tibet. Through diplomatic marriages he brought immeasurably significant cultural and spiritual enrichment to the country.

At the head of a well-organized army, the king in an expansionist drive plunged into the jungles of upper Burma and overran a large part of China. China at the time was acquiring a new dynasty, the Tang, and already had taken note of Tibet as the "Tu-fan" empire. A temporary peace was concluded between Tibet and China about A.D. 640, and King Songtsen Gampo received the Chinese princess, Wen Chen, in marriage. She became his second wife, since he had already married a Nepalese princess. Both wives were ardent Buddhists and highly cultured; each brought her own customs and manners to Tibet.

Chinese annals, in describing the warrior power of the unified Tibetans, expressed some astonishment at their fast-riding horses and the quality of their weapons. One account reported: "They clothe their entire body in armor, except for eye-holes. Even powerful bows and keen blades can do them little harm." Another related: "They have bows and swords, shields, spears, suits of armor and helmets. . . ." As for Tibetan civilization, the Chinese tended to characterize it as crude; they usually dismissed as sorcery the Tibetan religion of early times. Tibetans thought of themselves as wild and fierce, even barbarous.

King Songtsen Gampo initiated changes that, in time, tamed both the country and the people. Under the double influence of his wives, he built temples to house the sacred Buddhist images and began to study the religion on his own. He ordered a translation of the scriptures, including the "Hidden Great-

ness," and sent students and scholars to India and other lands
to work with Buddhist and Hindu teachers. An alphabet was
devised at his request with a script of thirty characters based
largely on an alphabet then used in Kashmir. This gave Tibet a
unified written language, even though the spoken dialects
differed from area to area. In the family of world languages,
Tibetan came to be classified in the Tibeto-Burmese grouping,
with its structure related to Burmese. Within a couple of decades, the alphabet was adapted to the language through use of
complicated orthography. The Tibetans even had a compre-
hensive grammar.

King Songtsen Gampo imported brocades and silks and mul-
berry trees from China, as well as the art of pottery making
and other skills. From India he imported Buddhist scholars and
gurus and their climate of spiritual development. The country
was open to outside influences, probably more so at this time
than later in its history. When the king decided that the
ancient capital of Yarlung in the south of Tibet was too remote
from the center of the consolidated nation, he moved it to
Lhasa. There he built a fort on top of a hill, the site of the
future Potala, a gigantic structure that ranks as a kind of
Oriental Vatican.

But King "Straight-Strong-Deep" is most revered for the
strong religious impetus he gave to the country. He openly
favored Buddhism and gave a beginning to this faith, though
by no means did he convert the nation as a whole. Later, the
people recognized him as an incarnation of their own Chenrezi.
At death, legend says, he dissolved into that patron-deity's
statue.

It should be explained that the religion of Tibet that flourished early was Bön, a curious mixture of exorcism and primitive nature worship. Bön leaders did not take kindly to the
introduction of Buddhism; eventually, however, some characteristics of this belief were absorbed into the Buddhism that
Tibetans embraced and which became their own Lamaism.

Bön recognized three regions inhabited by different classes

of beings: Heaven, the abode of gods and demi-gods; the earth, populated with humans and animals; and the underworld, filled with ghosts and demons. Gods were perceived as mild, beneficial creatures or as wrathful, damaging ones. Which aspect emerged depended on the individual and his attitude toward that god; in any case, the proper ritual could tip the scales in his favor. There were many rituals, and blood sacrifices were frequently offered. Some of the details were set down by Chinese observers. Animals were ordinarily the victims, but in earliest times even human beings had been offered. Bön followers believed that humans could be possessed by bad spirits, so "shamans" or priests had to perform rites to exorcise the spirits that could cause sickness and insanity. And everywhere there were *"lha"* or temporary godly spirits to be appeased. If a high pass had to be crossed, for example, then the spirits of the place must be bribed with offerings of stones or a prayer flag or something else significant. Though Bön went through different stages of development, it remained allied with much that was sorcery and magic. It did, however, advance some concept of rebirth.

The successor to Tibet's first historical king was Trisong Detsen, who, with the help of Indian Buddhist teachers, founded the first monasteries of the country. One of these teachers, known in India as Padmasambhava, came to be revered and honored in Tibet as the "Precious Teacher." Many stories were told of how this master "tamed" native demons hostile to Buddhism and to Tibet; how he made water flow from solid rock; that he could summon chariots from the sky. His occult powers made Bön "shamans" look weak by comparison, and he is credited with being the first great propagator of Buddhism in Tibet.

The last of the Buddhist kings under the country's ancient monarchy was Ralpachen, who ruled during the early half of the ninth century. He initiated many important reforms, including the introduction of a system of weights and measures and coins patterned after Indian models. His zeal in promoting

Buddhism and in giving gifts and privileges to its clergy won him enemies, and in the end he was assassinated. While the kings championed the new religion, many of the nobility favored the established Bön practices and objected to changes and reforms.

In external politics, Tibet had entered a kind of "Golden Age." Between Tibet and China a series of frontier conflicts had culminated in the dispatch of a Tibetan army, recorded as 200,000 men, against the Chinese. This wide-ranging venture led to the famous treaty of A.D. 821, written on a stone pillar at Lhasa. The Chinese and Tibetan text is still well preserved. It spelled out the relationship and fixed the frontiers between the countries at the time. In part, this remarkable agreement reads: "The Great King of Tibet . . . and the Great King of China . . . being in the relationship of nephew and uncle, have conferred together for the alliance of their kingdoms. . . . Tibet and China shall abide by the frontiers of which they are now in occupation. All to the east is the country of Great China; and all to the west is, without question, the country of Great Tibet. Henceforth on neither side shall there be waging of war nor seizing of territory. . . . Between the two countries no smoke nor dust shall be seen. There shall be no sudden alarms, and the very word 'enemy' shall not be spoken. Even the frontier guards shall have no anxiety or fear and shall enjoy land and bed at their ease. All shall live in peace and share the blessing of happiness for ten thousand years. The fame of this shall extend to all places reached by the sun and the moon. This solemn agreement has established a great epoch when Tibetans shall be happy in the land of Tibet and Chinese in the land of China. . . ."

The treaty appears to have fixed the boundary at a place not far west of the Chinese provinces of Kansu and Shensi.

Within Tibet, events became turbulent. A coup led by one faction of the nobility put on the throne Lang Darma, a man Tibetan annals depict as one of the most wicked ever born. He was cruel and "given to wine," according to written records, and began a merciless persecution of the Buddhists. He destroyed temples and forced Buddhist leaders to flee the country. He named anti-Buddhist noblemen to high government posts. How this ruler came to his deserved end is, once again, one of those wondrous Tibetan tales. He was assassinated by a phantom rider—a monk in disguise—who was urged in a vision to perform the deed. Ingeniously, the assassin blackened his white horse with charcoal, sooted his own face, and donned a black cloak. The monk rid Tibet of Lang Darma by shooting an arrow through the ruler's chest. The monk escaped, after swimming across a stream that washed out the charcoal and soot, making him unidentifiable as the assassin.

After the death of Lang Darma, two young children were set up as claimants to the throne, each supported by different factions of the nobility. The country broke down into a number of disunited princedoms and feuding principalities, and a dark age descended. The disintegration began about A.D. 842.

For some two centuries, little of a definite nature is known about religious, social and political conditions in Tibet. It was a time of civil strife and anarchy from which was to emerge the new ruling power of Tibet: religious hierarchies. What essentially stabilized the country was the revival of Buddhism in a movement called the Tibetan Renaissance, the "New Spread of Buddhism" as distinct from the "Old Spread" before the persecution under Lang Darma. When Buddhism made its comeback, there was, rather surprisingly, little animosity or bitterness between Bön and Buddhist believers, probably because Bön had lost some of its fierce characteristics and had absorbed some of the practices of its rival. The existing Buddhist monasteries and new ones that sprang up became symbols of refuge and security because they were built like fortresses. They represented places of safety in a country torn by wars between independent chiefs who battled for supremacy.

The outstanding spiritual figure in the Tibetan Renaissance was a Buddhist teacher from Bengal named Pandit Atisha who carried out an active, fruitful ministry throughout the country.

He arrived in Tibet about A.D. 1042 at the age of sixty and died there seventeen years later. He founded the Kadampa sect, which was to become the famous Gelukpa order, the reform sect of later centuries and the official sect of the Dalai Lamas.

This was a time of fervor and ferment, a time that bred extraordinary luminaries whom Tibetans considered saints, among them Milarepa, the "Cotton-clad"—so called because he wore only a simple cotton garment. A poet, troubadour, yogi and ascetic, he is equated with the Catholic St. Francis. His life showed Tibetans a new path—a life of compassion and renunciation.

CHAPTER THREE

Legacy of a
Hundred Thousand Songs

RELIGIOUS scriptures in Tibet are read and recited by monks, histories are read and quoted by scholars and some laymen, but the biography of Milarepa and his own "Hundred Thousand Songs" is read, repeated and loved by all Tibetans. Milarepa uniquely expressed his spiritual progress in songs, some lyrical, others mystic, still others amusing, and all quite philosophic. Here, in a segment from one of his songs, the sinner-turned-sage introduces himself:

I am Milarepa.
I am he who goes his own way;
I am he who has counsel for every circumstance;
I am the sage who has no fixed abode.
I am he who is unaffected whatever befall;
I am the alms-seeker who has no food;
I am the naked man who has no clothes;
I am the beggar who has no possessions.
I am he who takes no thought for the morrow;
I am he who has no house here nor dwelling there;
I am the victor who has known consummation.
I am the madman who counts death happiness;
I am he who has naught and needs naught.

Milarepa lived in the latter half of the eleventh century. He spent much of his life as a hermit in an area of arctic temperatures clad only in a thin cotton garment, subsisting on parched barley, roots and herbs, free from all material possessions and worldly quests. He sought and found enlightenment not through scholarship or knowledge but through direct perception and self-discipline. His life story was set down with simplicity and directness but in great detail by a disciple named Rechung. This biography, along with the songs Milarepa composed, rank as part of the national literature of Tibet.

Milarepa was born in a district near the frontier of Nepal. His father happened to be away at the time but was so pleased at the news that he named his son the Tibetan equivalent of "Delightful to Hear." The name turned out to be prophetic, since the son developed such a fine voice and talent for singing. The family was well off, and as a child Milarepa remembered having his hair plaited with gold and turquoises.

But all this changed with the death of his father when Milarepa was only seven years old. He and his mother and sister were cheated out of their property and their inheritance by a wicked uncle and aunt. The destitute family were compelled to work in the summer as laborers in the fields and in the winter as spinners and carders of wool.

"Our clothing was miserable rags tied to our bodies with a rope for a girdle," Milarepa is quoted as later telling his biographer. "Compelled to work without respite, our hands and feet became cracked and blistered. The insufficiency and coarseness of our food made us miserably emaciated and haggard. Our hair, once adorned with gold and turquoises, now became hard and stiff, and infested with lice."

Rather understandably, the mother wanted revenge and goaded her son into seeking out a sorcerer from whom he could learn the "black arts" and bring destruction to his uncle's household. Milarepa learned the arts well enough to bring down a house, killing thirty-five people, and to destroy a barley crop by conjuring a hailstorm. The deeds satisfied his mother's thirst for revenge but left Milarepa horror-stricken and seeking penance.

Milarepa sought out a teacher called Marpa, known as the Translator, who had studied in India and translated Buddhist works into Tibetan. For penance, Marpa set Milarepa a series of hard tasks, and to test the sinner's faith and devotion Marpa sometimes flew into a temper and treated his disciple almost unbearably. In despondency, Milarepa even ran away from Marpa several times, but he always came back. Finally the teacher, assured of his disciple's sincerity, initiated him into the doctrines of so-called tantric Buddhism. Together, so it is recorded, the teacher and disciple drank wine from a cup made from a human skull, an emblem of temporality used in tantric rites.

The teachings transmitted by Marpa were based on the belief that the powers of nature could invoke life and death in all beings and things; he used established symbols and figurative diagrams to convey his message. Just what was conveyed and exactly how remains mystifying. Of this direct oral transmission of doctrine from master to disciple much, apparently, must remain a secret. The system of ritual, however, stressed the value of meditation and control of mind and body through yoga practices. It led Milarepa to spend some six years in solitude and meditation in a cave.

Then Milarepa traveled to his birthplace, having seen in a dream the family house in ruins, his mother dead and his sister roving friendless in the world. All this turned out to be true, and, overcome with remorse, Milarepa decided to follow a life of complete reparation and severe asceticism. His initial period of self-denial in hidden mountain retreats was a bit too savage, for it reduced Milarepa to this self-described state: "My body was emaciated by the privations and hardships; my eyes were deeply sunken into the sockets; my bones showed prominently; my color was of a bluish-green; my muscles were all shrunken and shrivelled; a growth of bluish-green hair covered my skeleton-like form; the hairs of my head were stiff, and formed

a formidable wig; and my limbs appeared as if they were about
to break. Altogether, I was a sight which inspired . . . dreadful
fright."

He gradually eased some of his excessive self-discipline and
occasionally departed from his ordinary diet of nettles to accept other food. He attracted disciples, taught the faith, im-
parted wisdom through his songs, and worked wonders.
Because he had mastered the yoga of "inner heat," he needed
no more than a light cotton robe to withstand the extreme
cold, and is even supposed to have developed a power for
suspending himself in midair. His six best-known caves were
on the Tibet-Nepal frontier some 150 miles northwest of Mt.
Everest, according to historical Tibetan sources.

When Milarepa died at eighty-four years of age, the story
is told, the sky took on prismatic colors and symbolic patterns;
showers of blossoms descended, and gods came to walk among
men. Whether or not this was true, the poetry of Milarepa's
life seemed to continue even in his death.

To his disciples, the hermit-saint preached a message best
summarized in one of his verses:

> Dwell alone and ye shall find a friend;
> Take the lowest place and ye shall reach the highest;
> Hasten slowly and ye shall soon arrive;
> Renounce all worldly goals and ye shall reach the highest
> goal. . . .

To the average Tibetan, Milarepa's message was one of compassion and humility, the need to realize the illusive nature of
all things and the efficacy of good deeds, words and thoughts.

Overall, the Buddhism of Tibet tended to follow the so-
called truth of the middle way, which shunned excesses at any
level, either of self-indulgence or of self-mortification. It took
root from the Great Vehicle or Mahayana Buddhism which
intertwined deities, superhuman beings, rituals and personal
devotion. The emphasis was on "right" views and abstention

from evildoing through a path of right understanding, right thought, right speech, right actions, right livelihood, right effort, right mindfulness and right concentration.

Tibetans believed in different forms of existence, the highest being the realm of Buddha, where Nirvana or final bliss is attained. Human beings were on the scale somewhere between the higher forms and the lower ones, where suffering existed. A believer had to be born and reborn in a continual transmigration of soul or mind before reaching the highest form. Fortunately, or sometimes unfortunately, this change of abode from one tabernacle to another was based on *karma* or accumulated actions that earned merits or demerits. Transmigration was part of the theory that all things were constantly in flux. To be spared the "misery" of being born and reborn, the goal was to reach Nirvana.

Tibetan Buddhism took on the particular form of Lamaism from the very vital role of the "lama" or priest-teacher, around whom religious activity centered. To accumulate merits, the ordinary Tibetan looked to the monks and monasteries for assistance. The good actions of lay people could consist of making gifts to the monasteries and the lamas, making pilgrimages to the monasteries and asking lamas for blessings or favors. Extremely important in the Tibetan tradition was the ideal of a monk's achieving his own liberation, only to renounce it and return to the earth for the benefit of others. These were the "incarnations," which varied in importance. The highest came to rank as Tibet's god-king.

Lamaism developed into a complex and intricate system, with its own philosophical dialectics and metaphysics, its different aspects of yoga, its numerous rituals, popular traditions, literature, and systems of divination. Though its concepts were based on Indian Buddhism, the Tibetan offshoot included some beliefs and practices of the early Bön religion, with its magic storytelling and strange rites, and even added a bit of Hinduism. There was room for different paths to "enlightenment," for sophistry and primitive worship, for oracles and sacred scriptures, and for exorcists and ascetics like the truly revered Milarepa. In its effective establishment, Tibetan Buddhism was building not just a spiritual kingdom but a strong secular one as well.

CHAPTER FOUR

Tibet and the Mongol Rulers

ALREADY, in the eleventh century, Tibetan civilization was taking on the basic aspects it was to retain until modern times. History was no longer dealing with kings but with monasteries and religious hierarchies, supported by lay chieftains and nobility. Though still weak and divided, the country faced no outside threats. China, after the fall of the Tang dynasty in 906, appeared uninterested in Tibet. But a threatening power was in the making to the northeast of Tibet, in the land of the Mongols.

Within Tibet, a large monastery that was to assume both political and religious importance was founded in 1071, taking its name, Sakya, from the gray-colored earth on which it stood. It was located west of Shigatse, about halfway to the Tibet-Nepal border. Certain famous noble clans supported Sakya, and historic annals say that "the line upheld the school of tantric mysticism as well as the philosophical teachings of Mahayanist Buddhism." Celibacy for monks was not required, so it became a custom for the post of abbot to stay in the family, passing from father to son and other relatives. From

Sakya came the young abbot who was to carry Tibetan religious teachings to the Mongols.

At the beginning of the 1200s, Tibetans became aware of the might of the Mongols under the banner of Genghis Khan as the fierce horsemen began to overrun Asia and parts of Europe. They spilled into the eastern lands of Tibet but never actually occupied the country. The Tibetans wisely decided they had better establish definitive relations with this power. By this time Tibetans no longer had any political-military influence on the Asian scene. They were a passive people, subdued in no small part by Buddhism.

About 1245 a descendant of Genghis Khan named Godan, who was helping to consolidate Mongol influence in central Asia, heard about the powerful Sakya sect in Tibet and asked its reigning head to visit his court. Sakya Pandita went to the court, taking with him his nephew and eventual successor, Phakpa ("the Saint"). Different motives are ascribed to the Mongolian chief for his interest in Tibetan spiritual leaders, but it appears that he needed a learned lama at that time to invent a system of writing for the Mongols, whose language was only oral. This task was undertaken, and a kind of priest-patron relationship set in. The Sakya head advised the spiritual and temporal lords of Tibet to bow in submission to the Mongol dynasty. Actually, there was no other course, for the Mongols could and did send in their forces at different times. The Sakya sect, with the support of the Mongols, gained political power over the greater part of Tibet.

By 1280 the Mongols had completed their conquest of China, and Kublai Khan, grandson of Genghis, became the first Mongol emperor of all China. He summoned Phakpa to his imperial court. The celebrated lama won his respect by debating and defeating Nestorian, Mohammedan and Taoist theologians from China. The emperor declared Lamaism the national religion of his empire and the young lama his "imperial preceptor." What an unusual pair they must have been, this feared ruler of a vast empire and the cultured spiritual teacher from Tibet. Many titles were heaped on the lama, and he was proclaimed political ruler of his country. By this time Mongol armies had subdued any remaining power among Tibetan chiefs.

The Sakya supremacy initiated rule by grand lamas and merged religion with the state in Tibet. A central administrative system was organized, with the country divided into thirteen provinces of some 10,000 homesteads each, under rule of a lay governor. Internationally, the Sakya sect managed acceptable relations with two powerful neighbors, Mongolia and China.

Tibet had a special place in Mongol strategy because of the political and ideological roles its religion could fulfill. While Mongolia had military superiority, it lacked the sophistication of its neighbors, especially in religion. The Mongols themselves, once they had accepted Lamaism, did so with such intensity that they too came to lose their warring spirit. Tibet fittingly served as priest to its patron and protector, the Mongol dynasty.

China eventually revolted against Mongol rule, and the famous Ming dynasty was founded. Nominally, control over Tibet passed from the former Mongol emperors to the Chinese Ming rulers. But the practice of inviting leading Tibetan lamas to the imperial court and renewing their appointments, honors and titles continued. The Ming dynasty essentially maintained the same policy toward Tibet as had the Mongol emperors.

Within Tibet, the crumbling of Mongol might signaled the waning of power of the Sakya dynasty. Its political authority was questioned by other sects and independent monasteries, and dissension developed within the order itself. Noble families and a lay hegemony gained power. Overall, administration became fragmented and confused.

Different religious sects vied for favors and support with what were termed "tribute" missions. Tibetan monks traveled to the imperial court carrying gifts and blessings, then returned with silks, porcelains and other rich offerings. Chinese annals record that complaints began to crop up about the frequency of these missions, which sometimes involved the transporting of more than a thousand people. In 1569 an imperial Chinese edict reduced the missions to once every three years, limited the number of people in the retinue, and specified routes to be followed.

During its regency the Sakya dynasty had acquired immense wealth—much of it from the imperial court—and the monastery became a repository for vast religious treasures, among them golden statues and rich brocades. This wealth helped breed laxity and corruption, and the dynasty began disintegrating. There was need for reform and unity, and a commanding reformer did come in—"the Man from the Land of Onions," Tsong Khapa. He pushed monastic reform and discipline and founded the austere and historically important Gelukpa sect.

Tsong Khapa was born of nomadic parents in the Amdo district. He began religious training at a monastery while very young and took vows of monkhood as soon as he could. At sixteen, he was sent to study in the great monasteries of central Tibet. Tsong Khapa became both a thorough scholar and a forceful teacher, and he was an example to others by his own life.

Apparently he decided it was a losing battle to try direct cleansing or reformation of the older religious sects, so at about the age of fifty he started his own monastery, called Ganden ("The Joyous"), southeast of Lhasa. His followers came to be known as *Gelukpa* or "those who follow the virtuous way." They also were called the "Yellow Hats." It was the custom for monks to wear red hats, but Tsong Khapa, to set his followers apart, adopted yellow ones. Yellow was the color which Tibetans associated with purity and growth.

The zealous reformer demanded celibacy from all monks who joined the Gelukpa order, from the lowest to the highest. Most of the existing orders permitted marriage or intercourse for the lower orders of monks, and there are records of cases of debasing sensuality, particularly in the name of "tantric" experience. Tsong Khapa insisted on high academic standards as a prerequisite to advanced spiritual practice. He also required retreat periods for all members to constantly remind them of their spiritual goal. He introduced a grading of vows—a staggering 253—with each grade requiring more renunciation. But even this successful reformer could not erase the magic, wonder and occultism of Tibetan Buddhism, so he tended to linger on the symbolic meanings, rather than the literal practice, of the more esoteric beliefs and teachings. Basically, the central part of Gelukpa doctrine stressed the so-called Three Precious Truths—the Buddha, His Word and the Monkhood.

Some secular leaders and other religious sects were skeptical about the reform movement—and rather afraid of it—but the "Yellow Hats" attracted an ever-growing number of aspirants. Two other major monasteries were founded to house the growing ranks of monks; these were named Sera ("Wild Rose Fence") and Drepung ("The Rice Heap"). Both were close to Lhasa and, with Ganden, came to form the "Big Three" monasteries. Even in outward appearance, these monasteries differed from older ones. The Gelukpa-inspired centers were built in valleys, unlike the established ones which were perched on mountaintops, like fortresses.

There was no question that the Gelukpas were emerging as a new power in Tibet, taking over the previous eminence of the Sakya sect. Two other main sects existed: the Nyingmapa (meaning The Old) and the Karmapa, a subdivision of the Kagyupa which earlier had been founded by Marpa the teacher of Milarepa. Under the Ming rulers, the Karmapa sect appeared to be singled out for imperial favor and gifts.

Tsong Khapa too had received an invitation to visit the imperial court, but he refused. His reason was that if he made the trip with the large retinue traditionally expected, it would cause too much hardship to people along the route because they would contribute food and money which they themselves needed. The reformer, however, did send a representative, but to expound his teachings, not to solicit material support. The sect never won the full favor or support of the imperial court.

In a land where religious hierarchies rather than political parties determined the course of history and the fate of the country, the Gelukpas were destined for unusual service. The concept of the Dalai Lama, a new dynasty propagated by incarnation and succession, evolved from this sect.

CHAPTER FIVE

The Rise of God-Kings

AFTER the death of the great reformer in 1419, the mantle of Gelukpa leadership eventually fell to a gifted scholar named Gedun Truppa ("The Excellent One"). Like Tsong Khapa, he was the son of a herdsman from eastern Tibet. The story is told that, after he was born in a cattle pen, some robbers attacked the place, and his mother hid her baby in a heap of stones. Returning the next morning, she found the infant safe, guarded from all danger by a large raven. At the age of seven the boy entered monastic life, and at twenty he took the full vows of monkhood. His accomplishments were many, including the founding of the large monastery called Tashi Lhunpo ("Mountain of Blessings"), which later housed the spiritual leader Tibetans call Panchen Rimpoche, who was second in esteem only to the Dalai Lama. At Gedun Truppa's death it was assumed he passed into Buddhahood, with this description given: "His body, his illusory body, shrank a little owing to fatigue, and then suddenly shone with such brilliance that one could hardly look at it. The light turned into red and gold, white and gold, and then into pure gold." Gedun Truppa was Tibet's first Dalai Lama.

Soon after his death, the system of incarnation from man to man evolved. The belief that from time to time gods took birth in human form was not new. But the theory of successive reincarnation on a human level—that the first Dalai Lama himself returned in the body of another person—was new. Gedun Truppa, after all, had reached the state of enlightenment or Buddhahood; he had been released from the rounds of rebirth and could retire to the particular heaven to which he was entitled. Yet he chose to come back in another human body.

The religious authority of such a leader was not to be disputed. The Gelukpas had found the answer to perpetuating the leadership of their own sect and, as it developed later, effected a fusion of temporal and spiritual authority that was to make Tibet a theocracy.

At this period, however, the Gelukpas did not have secular power. Politically, the country was torn by feuds and quarrels among ruling families and by princes vying for leadership, backed by different monasteries. The Pagmotru family and its descendants ruled from Lhasa for several generations, with one of their group—Changchub Gyaltsen—becoming virtual ruler of all Tibet by 1350. Through internal strife, this lay hegemony went into decline toward the middle of the fifteenth century. Then the Rimpung princes seized power. They lasted only until the princes of Tsang, patronized by the Karmapas, became strong enough to take over in about 1565. They ruled from Shigatse. Administratively it was a confusing period. Socially it was a turbulent time; a variety of local uprisings were launched in which monasteries often became targets for attack.

Weakened and nearly spent by political and religious quarrels, Tibet needed a unifying force. What more appropriate healer for this disjointed land than a god-king? Yet it was not until the 1600s that god-kings became the undisputed sovereigns of Tibet, exercising supreme secular and spiritual authority. Before that time the Dalai Lamas were recognized as the sole incarnate successors to leadership of the Gelukpas and as living Buddhas.

The first Dalai Lama "came back" in the person of Gedun Gyatso, who further extended the size, influence and impact of the Gelukpa sect, continuing the work already begun. Although the sect still had no political power, it did develop an extensive internal administration of its own. When he died some seventy years later, Gedun Gyatso expressly stated that he wanted to return in a new body to advance the work further. The third in this succession of spiritual sovereignty was Sonam Gyatso, who showed a superhuman proficiency in his education and training and managed to perform miracles as well. Stories of his unusual powers reached as far as Mongolia, and he was invited to visit the court of the ruler, Altan Khan. He declined the first invitation but accepted the second, having become convinced of the vast opportunity to spread his religion in Mongolia. Tibetan Buddhism had been introduced in the country, but Mongolians tended to lean toward practices similar to those of the Bön religion in Tibet. To hold the attention of Mongolians, Sonam Gyatso demonstrated a few magical powers. He did this, en route to the court, by reversing winds, changing the climate, and even commanding a raging stream to flow backward up a mountainside. Or so Tibetan accounts relate.

The doctrinal message of Sonam Gyatso prompted Altan Khan to conversion. The Khan also proclaimed Tibetan Buddhism the national religion of Mongolia. To honor his spiritual mentor, the Altan Khan bestowed upon him the title, "Dalai Lama." "Dalai" was the Mongolian word for the Tibetan *gyatso*, meaning "ocean," and the designation translated to "Ocean of Wisdom." This title gained popularity in China and throughout the world, but Tibetans among themselves call

their leader Gyalwa Rimpoche ("Victorious One"). The
Mongolian title was extended retrospectively to the first incarnations and has been held by each successor in line.

Sonam Gyatso traveled widely in Mongolia and also visited
China. The reforged spiritual ties between Tibet and Mongolia
were not particularly pleasing to the Chinese, whose weaken-
ing Ming dynasty eventually gave way to the Manchus. Mongolia still represented a political force in the East. Within
Tibet, the Chinese had given their patronage to the Tsang
rulers, and they distrusted the growing influence and prestige
of the Gelukpas and their leaders.

Relations between Tibet and Mongolia became even firmer
when a grandson of Altan Khan, Yonten Gyatso, was recognized as the Fourth Dalai Lama. Yonten Gyatso took his preliminary studies in Mongolia before leaving to assume his duties
in Tibet. This development caused the Tsang rulers, whose
realm came to include all central Tibet, to feel more threatened
than ever by the "Yellow Hats" and their Mongol supporters.
Mounting tensions led to a widening range of conflict, including raids on Gelukpa monasteries.

An invasion dispatched in support of the Gelukpas by the
Mongolian prince Gushi Khan engaged and defeated the Tsang
forces, putting an end to the conflict. The conquest also put
an end to the existing political system. Gushi Khan in 1642
formally handed over control of the country to the Fifth Dalai
Lama, Ngawang Lobsang Gyatso, who truly inaugurated the
reign of god-kings as the supreme secular and religious sovereigns of Tibet.

Through diplomacy, religious strength and a gift for administration, this god-king, called the "Great Fifth," firmly
established the office of the Dalai Lama as an institution. There
was nothing like it anywhere in the world.

Altogether, there have been fourteen Dalai Lamas. They
have been searched out and found according to the same general pattern. Except for the incarnation from the Altan Khan
family, all have come from humble circumstances. Some have

emerged as exceptional leaders, but others were only mediocre. At least one was addicted to wine, women and song. A series of Dalai Lamas did not live long enough to make much political impact; between the intensely religious Eighth and the eminent Thirteenth, no Dalai Lama lived for more than twenty-three years. Yet the concept of the Dalai Lama has left an indelible mark, and not just in Tibet.

Tibetans regard their Gyalwa Rimpoche as an incarnate manifestation of their own all-compassionate patron deity, Chenrezi. As this Buddha commands their highest loyalty and devotion, the Dalai Lama commands like regard. The search to find a god-king is painstaking and time-consuming. There are definite paths taken. Evidence is checked, double-checked and counter-checked to guard against any possible fraud, because in the course of centuries there have been attempts to advance fraudulent candidates.

When a Dalai Lama dies, Tibetans say he *shingla gshegs pa* ("goes to the abode of gods for the benefit of other beings"). The search for his incarnation begins almost at once, for they believe that he reappears as a newborn child within a year. All Tibet offers prayers and invocations for the return of their god. In this "leaderless" period, a regent is appointed to govern the country until the new god-king is discovered and grows to maturity, to assume his full office at the age of eighteen.

There appear to be three basic steps to discovery of a Dalai Lama. First, it is determined whether clues—for example, as to which region of the country the new Dalai Lama would be found—have been left before or after the passing of the "old" incarnation. The next step is to seek indications through oracles, visions and other arts of divination. The third step is to follow up on these revelations through carefully chosen scouting parties, which are instructed to make certain tests to single out the incarnation.

Sometimes a Dalai Lama indicates where he is likely to take rebirth. When the Third Dalai Lama neared death in Mongolia, he was beseeched by Mongolian princes to return among

them to continue his spiritual mission. He assured them this was
his wish too, and the next Dalai Lama was found in Mongolia.
The Sixth Dalai Lama suggested in a verse he wrote that he
would return from a place called Litang. This proved to be the
case. After the Thirteenth Dalai Lama died, his body was found
turned to the east. His incarnation was discovered in Amdo in
eastern Tibet.

Oracles are consulted as a matter of course, the most important being the State Oracle of Nechung. These oracles,
actually monks who act as mediums, go into a trance to com-
municate mysterious and hidden answers to specific questions.
They are asked to provide some particulars about the new
god-king. Different lakes exist in Tibet where, allegedly, the
future can be read, and one special "oracle lake" called Lhama
Lamtso, southeast of Lhasa, is always consulted for guidance
in locating a new Dalai Lama. It was in the still waters of this
lake, for example, that officials on the hunt for the Fourteenth
Dalai Lama "saw" the setting and small house where the god-
king was to be found, along with the letter A, taken to mean
Amdo.

The search parties dispatched to find the new Dalai Lama
consist of both monks and laymen. Their mission, carried out
as quietly as possible, sometimes takes two to three years. It is
a singular adventure known to Tibetans as "making the recognition." Members of these search parties disguise themselves
when approaching possible incarnations to make preliminary
tests. Sometimes more than one candidate emerges, because
the Buddhist theory explains that every being has three outlets
of expression—body, speech and mind—and each may take a
separate incarnation. If this happens, the "incarnation of the
mind" is deemed the true incarnation.

The searchers carry with them actual possessions of the
former incarnation, together with similar-looking items which
are not his own, to determine whether the candidate can distinguish between them. True incarnations have snatched the
"valid" articles as their own. These incarnations—just toddlers

—have appeared to know their unexpected visitors, greeting them as friends. The searchers verify whether the birth of the child was accompanied by certain auspicious signs, such as the appearance of a rainbow in a clear sky. There are always distinct physical marks, including elongated eyes, eyebrows that curve upward on the outside, large ears, and specific imprints on the shoulder blades and palms of the hands.

When the authorities have examined all the evidence and are convinced that the true incarnation has been found, then the new Dalai Lama—as young as four or five years—is brought to Lhasa for the ceremony of enthronement. Dressed in rich robes and surrounded by lamas, high officials and invited guests, the youngster is lifted to the pedestal of his office in a vast hall known as the Great Throne Room, in the hallowed Potala. Then the highest lama comes forward to chant the "Prayer for the Power of the Golden Throne." The rites proceed, with entreaty, praise and devotion to symbolize the acceptance of the new Dalai Lama by the Tibetan nation. At the end of the ceremony, well-wishers approach the throne bearing the *khata*, a white scarf used in welcoming, and special gifts. The Dalai Lama gives each a blessing. The enthronement generates a period of rejoicing throughout all Tibet.

If there is some uncertainty about the true incarnation and several candidates are advanced, then selection can be by lottery, preceded by a particular consecration and special invocation of the gods. In 1792, during the overlordship of the Manchus in Tibet, the Chinese emperor decreed use of the so-called method of the golden urn for selection of the Dalai Lama. This consisted of writing the names of approved aspirants on slips of paper and drawing lots from a golden urn. Tibetans preferred to disregard this decree, but in later enthronements a golden urn was presented to the new Dalai Lama as a symbol of his office.

Once enthroned, the Dalai Lama begins an austere existence of training and discipline, prayers and ritual in which he learns the responsibilities of his future years as a spiritual and secular leader. He is separated from his parents and allowed only a small amount of time for a normal childish activity. His training is that of a lama, and more. Once he comes of age, his word and power are absolute.

The families of Dalai Lamas traditionally are honored with special titles and gifts that include grants of land, but according to custom no blood relative of the Dalai Lama can be appointed to any public office.

To the western mind, the entire concept of a god-king seems unreal, even startling, but Tibetans have a way of humanizing their gods while deifying human beings. They do not find it at all strange to have contact with incarnations of Buddhas and lesser deities. They have no difficulty accepting the idea that a Dalai Lama is a rebirth of the historical figure he was in a preceding life or that their own patron deity of Chenrezi is present in each succeeding Dalai Lama. They remember that this god made a vow to be born many times for the good of Tibet, to tarry until "all the sheep, down to the last, have been safely gathered within," according to a symbolic statement.

CHAPTER SIX

The Great Fifth and Merry Sixth

IN ONE OF those curious ironies of history, Tibet's most illustrious Dalai Lama, known as "the Great Fifth," was followed by the most notorious incarnation ever to hold the title. Tibetans dubbed the dissolute Sixth "the Merry One." Yet even earthly preoccupations by their god-king did not lessen the everyday Tibetan's belief in and regard for the institution of the Dalai Lama. If they complained at all, it was simply to suggest that the Sixth may have been sent to test their faith.

To the Great Fifth, modern Tibet seems to owe most of its secular and ecclesiastical makeup. Coming into power in 1642, he led the unification of the country and set the pattern of power for the office of the Dalai Lama. He showed a flair for statesmanship in relations with the Mongols and the Chinese. He proclaimed the festival of the Great Prayer, which served to unite the people and to demonstrate their spiritual fervor. He left behind an incredible monument, the Potala Palace, which came to symbolize to Tibetans and outsiders alike the uniqueness and grandeur of the country.

In foreign affairs, the Fifth Dalai Lama was quick to appraise the new political tides in China. There the Ming fiefdom had tottered and the Manchus had conquered China proper, to launch the Ching dynasty. The Great Fifth established relations with this new power, and in 1652 he himself went to Peking to visit the Manchu monarch. Lodged in a monastery built especially for the occasion, he spent nearly six months in the Chinese capital. It is recorded that the emperor descended from his dragon throne to meet the visitor as a sovereign of equal rank.

W. W. Rockhill, the well-known American diplomat, scholar and historian, describing this visit from primarily Chinese accounts, records: "He [*i.e.* the Fifth Dalai Lama] had been treated with all the ceremony which could have been accorded to any independent sovereign, and nothing can be found in Chinese works to indicate that he was looked upon in any other light; at this period in China's relations with Tibet, the temporal power of the Lama, backed by the arms of Gushi Khan and the devotion of all Mongolia, was not a thing for the Emperor of China to question."

The meeting renewed the patron-priest relationship between the countries, but the lamas in Tibet were not the sole beneficiaries of the arrangement. The Manchus themselves had a significant interest in maintaining a Manchu-Tibetan alliance. For them, the Tibetan nation, with its religious role, was seen as ideologically powerful in preventing the renewal of warlike qualities in their enemies, the Mongols.

Chinese recognition and patronage stretched to another outstanding Tibetan spiritual leader, the Great Fifth's former teacher, whom he named Panchen Rimpoche ("Precious Great Sage"). Successors of the Panchen Rimpoche became known in the world as Tashi Lamas. The Chinese honored him as a second Incarnate Lama and, in later centuries, connived to pit the Panchen Lama against the Dalai Lama in attempts to divide, influence and conquer Tibet.

Within Tibet, the Fifth Dalai Lama took a census of the monasteries and regulated their revenues and taxes. He sent representatives into troubled areas to reduce excessive taxation,

mediate local feuds, and preserve order. He founded schools
for the training of lay and monk officials and began other
pioneering reforms. The centralized form of government
created during the reign of the Great Fifth lasted, with little
change, until the modern era. Under this system, ultimate
power rested with the Dalai Lama, but general administration
of the government was subject to deliberation by monk-lay-
man units. Actual administration was carried on by a regent
who exercised much authority in secular affairs. The body
politic was built on the two pillars of religion and state. The
landlords of Tibet—the nobles and monasteries—shared in the
power and authority of government, having vast control over
their tenants.

In initiating the *Lhasa Mönlam* ("Great Prayer"), the Fifth
Dalai Lama enlarged Tibetan tradition, folklore and festivity.
The event marks the Tibetan new year, determined by the
capricious Tibetan calendar, which lags roughly one to one
and a half months behind the western calendar. The event
begins with a tremendous influx of people into Lhasa and a
general uproar of galloping costumed paraders, bell clanging
and shouting. Then come speeches, services, dramatic presen-
tations, other amusements, and almsgiving. By special edict
of the Fifth Dalai Lama, monks were made wardens of public
security during this tumultuous time, since Tibet did not have
—and has never organized—an established police force. The
Great Prayer and related ceremonies continue for weeks.
Religious art blossoms on huge wooden frames—sometimes
three stories high—showing Buddhist scenes and spiritual
symbols, all fashioned entirely of colored butter. This particular Lamaist art, extremely intricate and precise, evokes an
unreal, magical aura, especially when night falls and the gallery
of giant butter pictures is illuminated by butter lamps and gas
lights. But these extraordinary mosaics are short-lived; they
are melted in flames to demonstrate the transitory nature of
all things. Tradition has it that the religious butter-towers
were the outgrowth of a dream experienced by the Great Fifth.

In building the Potala, which was finished in 1694, the Fifth Dalai Lama left a landmark to the country's national culture. He made this structure the headquarters for the central government, moving administration from the Gelukpa monastery of Drepung in Lhasa. For the people, however, the Potala became a place of pilgrimage, representing for them the spiritual might of Tibet rather than its political power.

Like a Cyclops, the Potala dominates Lhasa. The white-faced structure soars some four hundred feet—blanketing an entire small mountain—with walls climbing upward, sloping inward from the base in a giant tiered birthday-cake arrangement. It is about one thousand feet long, with thousands of windows, powerful battlements and vast staircases shaping a distinctive facade. Within its thirteen stories, two palaces actually exist. The white section quarters the government and the upper central crimson-colored stories comprise the residence of the Dalai Lama. Almost a city in itself, the structure houses about one thousand rooms, including thirty-five chapels, a monastery, a school, a library, various treasuries of church items and relics, the tombs of Dalai Lamas, and various meeting halls. The Potala is accessible only through a confusing maze of corridors and up interminable flights of stairs. From the outside, the staircases give an appearance of being piled on top of one another. The entire building seems to defy simple description, but the leading Italian Tibetologist, Guiseppi Tucci, probably summarized it best. He called it "a craggy, truncated pyramid."

The construction itself seemed a miracle. It was built entirely of stone, every block of which had to be carted from the quarry to the site. The tedious job was done by hand by the workers, assisted only by beasts of burden. Construction took some fifty years; the Fifth Dalai Lama died before it was completed.

Also during the reign of the Great Fifth different travelers, scholars and traders reached Lhasa, among them Indians, Muslims, Chinese and Mongols, and all were welcomed. The first European visitors were Catholic missionaries; trade missions were to come later. Between 1624 and 1721 Jesuit missionaries came from different countries, the most famous being the Italian Ippolito Desideri, who learned Tibetan well enough to hold disputations on theology. The Capuchins came later, and both orders founded short-lived missions in Tibet.

Having set a vigorous and dynamic course for Tibet, the Fifth Dalai Lama decided to retire. He turned political power over to a capable regent, Sanggye Gyatso, who was rumored in some accounts to have been his natural son. Other annals deny this claim, maintaining that the Great Fifth did take full vows to lead a celibate life, as is expected of Dalai Lamas. In any event, the Dalai Lama went into religious seclusion and died in 1680. The regent, who wanted to keep the prestige, power and strong authority of the Great Fifth, managed for nine years to keep this news from the people. This seems rather an impossible feat until one considers the size of the Potala and the possibilities of his "vanishing" to live in spiritual solitude. Apparently, too, elaborate deceptions were employed. Meals, for example, continued to be delivered to the Dalai Lama's room, and officials standing outside the room could hear the continuous sounds of the hand drum and bell used in rituals, signifying that the Dalai Lama was deep in meditation. On state occasions a monk who looked like the Dalai Lama impersonated him, and these appearances started whispers about whether this really was the Great Fifth.

Finally the death of the Dalai Lama was announced. The Sixth Dalai Lama appears not to have been recognized until he was about ten years old. Thus Tsangyang Gyatso missed an early upbringing under monastery discipline. Seemingly it was too late to train him for the life and duties of an ascetic ruler. At the age of twenty he renounced his vows of celibacy but remained the Dalai Lama. He pursued the pleasures of worldly life with gusto. His haunts were certain yellow-washed houses in Lhasa where he cavorted with lady loves. Also, he liked to drink *chang*, a rice beer. According to a traditional account of his appearance, "The Merry One," bedecked with rings and jewels, his black hair somewhat long, wore the blue silk robe of a lay nobleman.

The Sixth Dalai Lama seemed utterly unfit for the high office. He led an austere enough life within the walls of the Potala, but his excesses outside made some authorities say that a true incarnation had not been found, that some mistake had been made. Yet he left some of the most lyrical poetry known to Tibetans. With charming descriptions of his escapades in town, it is quoted to this day among the ordinary people. The Sixth Dalai Lama aptly described himself in this short verse:

> I dwell apart in Potala
> A god on Earth am I;
> But in the town, the prince of rogues
> And boisterous revelry.

But not all of his verses were so light and frivolous, as evidenced by this poem, thoughtfully composed:

> What you write in ink, in small black letters,
> Can all be lost
> Through the work of a single drop of water.
> But what is written in your mind,
> Is there for eternity.

A council was held in which the leader of Mongol forces appealed to the leading lamas to depose him. The lamas expressed their view that the mode of the Sixth Dalai Lama's life stemmed from "no spirit of enlightenment." None suggested the possibility that he was not the true Dalai Lama. The people too believed in "The Merry One" as an incarnation, and some offered their own interpretation, which was that the Sixth Dalai Lama had the power to assume several forms, with one body anchored in Potala Palace and a secondary body used when carousing.

The emperor of China sided with the Mongol chiefs in

Tibet, and the situation gave the Chinese an excuse to attempt assurance of a more "fitting" leader and extend their influence over Tibetan affairs. The Dalai Lama was invited to Peking and mysteriously died en route. His death prompted as many stories as his life, with one version being that the Chinese murdered him when his party arrived at a certain lake.

Yet, in the end, the unusual Sixth seems to have outwitted his enemies. Before leaving Lhasa he made a strange proclamation which people later interpreted as a prediction of his rebirth. He said he saw a white crane flying east over the city and he sang this verse:

> White bird in the sky,
> Lend me but one great wing
> That I too may fly eastward;
> Soon I shall return, from Litang,
> And give you back your wing.

His incarnation was born in Litang in eastern Tibet and became known for his saintliness. But other candidates appeared or were promoted for the Dalai Lama's throne, and the authority of the Tibetan Buddhist church seemed threatened. Caught in a power struggle, Tibetans appealed to the Dsungars, a Mongolian tribe in remote northwestern Sinkiang, to help them defeat forces opposing the true incarnation. Although the Dsungar chief was related to the commander of Mongol forces in Tibet, he seized this opportunity for power. In the winter of 1717 Lhasa was conquered and the established Mongol commander and his followers defeated and killed. The Dsungars had already gained strength in central Asia, and the addition of Tibet to their domain could make them strong enough to challenge the Manchus. China decided they had to be defeated. Three years later, in 1720, a Chinese army entered Lhasa for the first time, and the occasion gave the Chinese an opportunity to establish some degree of civil and military administration in Tibet. A new period loomed in Tibetan history, an era of Manchu suzerainty.

CHAPTER SEVEN

Under the Manchus

FOR A period of almost 200 years, Tibet was recognized as a Manchu protectorate. The arrangement was flexible enough to be accepted by the Tibetan government, with Chinese influence fluctuating according to its "mandate from heaven." Never did Tibet become a part of Chinese territory.

But these were troubled centuries. There was internal strife, and there were threats from without. The Dalai Lamas, from the Eighth to the Twelfth, either died young or did not exert much political impact. Despite itself, Tibet got mixed up in big power politics because of its strategic position at the boundaries of three rival powers—China, British India and Czarist Russia. "The Hermit Kingdom" was not such a hermit by the time the Manchus were toppled.

At the beginning of the protectorate the Chinese recognized the Seventh Dalai Lama, and as early as 1723 they had withdrawn their troops from Lhasa. But they annexed a large slice of eastern Tibet, and after a revolt by a local prince in Koko Nor the whole region became the Chinese province of Chinghai. The territory of Tibet, handed down almost unaltered through the previous centuries, underwent a substantial reduction for the first time.

Serious dissension between pro-Manchu ministers in the government and "nationalist" adversaries led to a civil war in 1728, with another appearance of Chinese troops to restore peace. This internal crisis convinced the Manchus they needed to keep troops on Tibetan soil to protect their own position. They decided to station representatives, *ambans*, to look after the emperor's interest, in Lhasa, along with a garrison of 2,000 soldiers. These consuls did not rule Tibet, but their presence, backed by military power, had some influence on the final decisions of the Tibetan authorities. At this early stage, *ambans* were described as "little more than observers" by the eminent English historian of Tibet, H. E. Richardson.

From 1728 to 1734, the Manchus exiled the Seventh Dalai Lama from Lhasa to eastern Tibet and turned temporal rule over to their ally, Sonam Topgye of Phola, who had been one of the chief ministers. The Manchus believed that disruptive nationalist elements centered around the Dalai Lama; it was a fact that his father was involved in "nationalist" activities.

Sonam Topgye was given the title of "king" of Tibet, and he dominated Tibetan affairs until his death in 1747. A period of some normalcy was established, with the "king" showing both political reliability and diplomatic talents. After his reign, a son succeeded to the kingship who secretly tried to arrange an alliance with the Dsungars against the Manchus. He did convince the Manchus that the situation in Tibet had become so stabilized as to require only a small number of imperial troops in Lhasa. Once most of the troops were withdrawn, an anti-Manchu uprising broke out. During the fighting and confusion, the young king was decoyed into the residence of the *ambans* and murdered. The Tibetans, in turn, took revenge by killing the *ambans* and half their guards.

Once again—in what had become a fairly regular occurrence—the Manchu emperor sent in an expedition to take over Lhasa. The kingship was abolished, the government reorganized, and new *ambans* appointed. The Dalai Lama, whom the Manchus saw as only a religious leader, was restored to power.

But now stricter measures of control were exercised by the Chinese, with the *ambans* assuming a limited right of partici- pation in the government of the country. The Manchus tended to support the regents who ruled during the minority of a Dalai Lama. Strangely enough, regents represented the supreme government authority for about a hundred years, because suc- cessive Dalai Lamas never reached maturity. Tibetans were convinced that the Manchus had a hand in this development.

An outside threat temporarily drew attention away from the country's internal turmoil when, in 1788, the warlike Gurkhas south of the Himalayas invaded the country. The pretext was that Tibetans were fraudulently exporting goods from Tibet and taxing Gurkha merchandise. The Gurkhas defeated the Tibetans, who promised to pay a certain sum of money annually to the victors. When the Tibetans failed to pay, the invaders from Nepal attacked again in 1791. This time the Chinese came to the rescue, driving the attackers back to Nepal. The Manchu emperor decreed that control within Tibet had to be tightened and the country sealed off against foreign intervention. In 1792 Tibetan frontiers were closed and the Manchus initiated a thorough—and humiliating —political reform. The *ambans* took over frontier defenses, the administration of finances, and control of all foreign rela- tions and trade. The Dalai Lama and his ministers were pre- vented from acting independently of the Chinese consuls. This crackdown led to the effective economic, political and military isolation of Tibet from the outside world.

But the outside world was not to be kept at bay for long. A new power—the island empire of Great Britain—loomed on Tibetan mountain boundaries in the 1880s, anxious to pene- trate the "mysterious" land north of India in the name of trade and of protection of the Indian empire. British subjects had already entered Tibet on official and semiofficial missions, but no government relations existed between Tibet and Great Britain. British political activities which resulted in pulling the Himalayan hill states into their own orbit to secure the defense of the Indian empire did not inspire any trust from the Tibetans. The latter came into conflict with the British over Sikkim, which was religiously and ethnologically both a part of Tibet and a tributary state to China. In 1890 Tibet lost its position in Sikkim. An Anglo-Chinese agreement fixed the boundary between Sikkim and Tibet and established Britain's protectorate over Sikkim.

Tibet had now been dragged into the caprices of international politics. The British continued to make arbitrary decisions affecting Tibet, and in 1893 another Anglo-Chinese arrangement fixed regulations covering trade, communications, and pasturage rights along the Sikkim frontier. But British attempts to enforce the provisions met only with stolid refusal from the Tibetans, who practiced a kind of civil disobedience that paralyzed all trade.

When the British tried to protest directly to the Dalai Lama, their messages to him were returned unopened. The viceroy of India, Lord (George Nathaniel) Curzon, declared in 1902 that it was "the most extraordinary anachronism of the twentieth century that there should exist within less than 300 miles of the border of British India, a state and a government with whom political relations do not so much as exist and with whom it is impossible to exchange a written communication." He came to maintain that Chinese suzerainty over Tibet was "a constitutional fiction" and that this "political affectation had been maintained only because of its convenience to both parties."

During this period the Chinese were harassed by foreign penetration and by unrest at home and were in no position either to restrain the British or to keep Tibetans under control for negotiation. The Manchu dynasty was not destined to last much longer. Within Tibet, imperial power had declined, the strength of the Chinese garrisons had dwindled, and the *ambans* were exercising little authority. For all practical purposes, the protectorate of Manchu China over Tibet had become defunct.

While Tibet had generally managed to keep China at arm's length, the imperial power of Great Britain seemed to be another matter. Tibetan leaders began to look about for a strong new "patron" and turned some attention to Russia. The czar had expressed an interest in trade, but in reality he was interested in using Tibet as a convenient back door to China. A mysterious Russian, a Buriat Mongolian monk named Agvan Dorjiev, had become a close attendant of the Dalai Lama—the young Thirteenth—and managed to establish himself in Lhasa as an unofficial representative of the Russian government. Rumors circulated that the Russians would set up a consulate in eastern Tibet, and there was no question that the Dalai Lama had had secret interchanges with the Russian czar. The British saw Russia as a possible threat on the Asian continent, imperiling their empire interests. They pushed for direct talks in Lhasa to establish a permanent consular or diplomatic representative in Tibet. This way they hoped to end the political flirtation between Lhasa and St. Petersburg and to keep Tibet a buffer state.

The British sent in an armed mission under Col. Francis Edward Younghusband, dispatched with diplomatic aims. It started in peaceful penetration, but before it reached Lhasa on Aug. 3, 1904, there were bloody clashes with the Tibetans, who, although ill equipped and disorganized, put up some resistance. The expeditionary force included some 3,000 armed soldiers, and foreign critics later proclaimed that Tibetans were "shot down like partridges." It appeared to be a sorry chapter in British imperial history, though the English did then negotiate patiently and moderately with the Tibetans to reach some suitable agreement, withdrawing their troops as soon as the provisional signing of the treaty was finished. The Tibetan government recognized the British protectorate over Sikkim, agreed to trade with India, and promised to prevent other foreigners from gaining influence in Tibet.

The regent of Tibet led the country's negotiating group, since the Dalai Lama, with a small party, had fled to Mongolia before the advance of the western invaders. From there he went to Peking in 1908. The British advance seemed timed to the outbreak of the Russo-Japanese war in Manchuria, so that neither Chinese nor Russian intervention in Tibet was a possibility. China was still recovering from the Boxer rebellion.

Importantly, the Lhasa treaty of 1904 did establish the precedent of direct negotiation by England with Tibet and without consideration of China. It also recognized England as the most favored nation with "special interests" in Tibet. Moreover, Tibet opened new trade markets at Gyantse and Gartok. The country was pushed into greater commercial contact.

China was rudely awakened to the fact that Tibet was slipping away from her influence. She contrived the Peking convention of 1906 whereby she ratified the Lhasa treaty provisions but secured from Britain a provision that Tibet's internal administration and the preservation of her integrity should rest with China. To China, this represented a British admission of Chinese rights in Tibet. A year later the British signed yet another treaty, this time with Russia. The Russians acknowledged England's "special interests" in Tibet and agreed that the country should remain closed to all foreign penetration. This treaty used the word suzerainty to describe China's relationship to Tibet, suggesting that the Chinese had not exercised any real internal authority.

The implication helped to stir the Chinese to action again. They moved to consolidate their position in eastern Tibet, an unstable zone bordering on China's three inland provinces. The Manchu general, Chao Erh-feng (Tibetans dubbed him "The

Butcher"), annexed frontier land, took over any remaining authority from local chieftains, "pacified" the countryside, and established Chinese control in Lhasa.

Meanwhile, in 1909, the Thirteenth Dalai Lama had returned from the long exile during which he had lost Chinese imperial favor. He found his position untenable when a Chinese army 2,000 soldiers strong came marching into Lhasa. Along with several leading officials, he secretly escaped to India, where he passed another period of exile in the sanctuary of the former foe, the British government of India. Peking used the occasion to "depose" him. The year was 1910.

Thus, at the close of two turbulent centuries, Tibet was back at her starting point: under a Chinese squeeze. But the famous 1911 revolution in China settled the whole issue. The Manchus were overthrown, and yet another Chinese dynasty crumbled. Tibetans began to drive the Chinese out of their country, and the Dalai Lama, negotiating with the British in India, declared the independence of Tibet. This was to be a relatively short period of modern independence, for China once again, this time under Communist leadership, would deal the final blow to Tibetan freedom.

CHAPTER EIGHT

Lhasa: "God's Place"

A TIBETAN PROVERB says: "All roads lead to Lhasa." These roads beckoned not just visitors from the near and distant outside world but every resident of Tibet as well. To go to Lhasa truly meant, to the mass of Tibetans, a pilgrimage to "God's Place." This journey had to be made at least once by even the poorest and the humblest; it was a lifelong hope. For these travelers the fabled capital pulsated as the heart of their religion rather than as the nerve center of politics. Whatever their reason for visiting Lhasa, all guests—from home and abroad—seemed to agree that here was a destination which, once seen, would always be remembered. The reason for this was simple enough: No city like it existed anywhere else in the world.

By western standards of size, Lhasa ranks as a town and not a city. It lies in the broad, fertile valley of the Kyichu River, a tributary of the Tsangpo, and stretches only about two miles from east to west and less than one mile from north to south. It is located at an elevation of some 12,000 feet, with a mild, pleasant climate most of the year and a sky vividly and eternally blue. The city is circled by mountains perhaps 4,000 to 5,000 feet high from which some of the snow ranges of Tibet can be seen in the far distance. Lhasa's population is estimated at about 40,000, half being monks. At festival times the number of people in the city doubles.

Lhasa proper houses historic monuments, colorful bazaars, homes, shops, shrines and public buildings. The typical Tibetan style predominates, with low, rectangular-shaped, white-faced, sturdy construction showing sharp corners and rows of small window openings. The marketplace of Lhasa, at the east end, traditionally attracted not just traders but pilgrims as well, with much bustling and jostling in the small lanes crossing the section. Tibetans developed trading into a kind of art that all residents relished and enjoyed. Business in the marketplace could cover everything from daily food provisions to the purchase of mules. The stalls and shops spread before the admiring eyes of onlookers and buyers part of the wealth and luxury of central Asia: exotic furs, rich brocades, dazzling silks, oriental carpets, fanciful brass lamps and ornaments, precious jewels, leather saddles and spices and perfumes. Western goods, too, found their way to Lhasa in recent decades. The barter and bargaining could sound fierce, but once business was done, the "disputants" could laugh, joke and drink *chang* together.

In the heart of Lhasa, on an irregular square, stands the holy shrine, the Jokhang, associated with many legends and initiated during the reign of King Songtsen Gampo. A vast underground lake was supposed to have once existed under this cathedral, where visions of the future could be read. Destroyed and rebuilt at different times, this temple, over the centuries, served as a rallying point for Tibetan Buddhism and as the goal of millions of pilgrims. At the gate of the temple droops an ancient willow tree, said to have been planted by the Chinese wife of Songtsen Gampo. Lhasa residents call it "the Lord's Hair." Inside, the shrine is divided into a collection of chapels and corridors and a main assembly hall, with butter

LHASA TEMPLE
Roofs of the sacred Jokhang.

lamps burning continuously and celebrated images, mural paintings and ornate religious symbols reflecting the rich beauty of Tibetan church art. Pilgrims sometimes make their way around this shrine on their knees.

Everywhere in Lhasa there are holy places, and around the outskirts are monasteries both big and small. The Potala ("peak") looms solitary and majestic on its own hill at the north of the city, an imposing white and red fortress softened by its gilded roofs. In front of this headquarters a group of government buildings and offices of magistrates are found. Just behind the Potala, one of the most picturesque parts of the city is centered about a small lake which reflects the facade of the Potala and which is surrounded by plants, flowering shrubs and giant poplars. On an island in the middle of the lake rests a temple called the House of the Serpent.

The view from the Potala, not only of Lhasa and its environs but of the entire plain and the winding Kyichu ("Waters of Pleasure"), prompted rhapsodic comments from visitors, particularly westerners. But Tibetans who entered the Potala did so not for the satisfaction of sightseeing but as pilgrims or as persons on missions of government.

POTALA
The palace of the Dalai Lama.

Pilgrims climb steep steps on the rock-faced hill to reach the Potala and arrive at the main pilgrim's entrance. There they step into a dark chamber in which an immense prayer wheel, some twenty feet high and eight feet in diameter, greets them. Each pilgrim turns this wheel and a somber-toned bell sounds. From here the religious tour continues through dim corridors lit by butter lamps into a maze of passages and staircases. There are many shrines and temples to be visited; incomparable church relics to be revered; splendid examples of religious art to be seen; colossal tombs of the Dalai Lamas to be admired. These tombs, enclosed in *chörten* (a kind of pagoda), reach for the skies at the top of the Potala, and radiate into a golden canopy on the roof. The most important temple is dark and fairly small: the temple to Chenrezi, where the main image on the altar is not more than eighteen inches high. For pilgrims, a day is scarcely enough time for a satisfying visit. Many bring picnic meals with them.

The sections of the Potala painted white marked the secular government offices, residences for lay members of the staff, and a school for government officials. Government officials formed a kind of lay nobility. The prime duties of government were concerned with the lay population, since the monasteries and religious people had a separate authority and hierarchy. Under the supreme leadership of the Dalai Lama, every Tibetan was a subject of the church if he was a member of a sect; a subject of the state if he was not. The government tended to be "of God, by God and for God."

From his pinnacle in the Potala, the Dalai Lama could rule as he wished; for him there was no fixed pattern. Primarily, though, he concentrated on the spiritual welfare of the people in exercising his power as a lama or teacher. His power in non-spiritual affairs he delegated to a regent, usually an incarnate lama. The Dalai Lama worked with a series of councils, beginning with his own inner court. Since it was not customary for the Dalai Lama to have direct dealings in affairs of state, a liaison office called the "Front of the Peak" served as an intermediary between "His Holiness" and the outside world.

The highest administrative unit was the *Kashag,* in effect a cabinet, appointed from laymen and monks nominated by the national assembly or *Tsongdu.* The *Tsongdu* had no regular sessions; it was summoned when the cabinet wanted advice. In reality it was a consultative body and a forum, with no actual legislative function. It consisted of monk leaders, lay officials from the central government, and representatives of different professions and vocations.

A finance department was presided over by lay officials, with the treasury the most important part of this department. Tibet had only direct taxes, collected in the form of such goods as barley, cattle and cloth. Because monasteries and their properties were exempt from taxes, the population paying taxes was not too large and the rate tended to be high. From Lhasa, all land was divided into three main groups and all the people grouped according to the land from which they derived a living. The first was the estate of the church, including land granted to individual lamas; the second, public properties belonging to the state; and the third, family estates owned by the nobility and a small number of commoners subject to the state, church or nobility.

The Potala housed a private treasury for the Dalai Lama and a reserve treasury of precious stones and metals to be used only in a national emergency.

There appeared to be no separately organized judicial system, and a wide range of government officials could sit as courts of law. Cases could be appealed, with parties addressing themselves to the Kashag or even to the office of the Dalai Lama or his regent. Normal punishment was flogging, but it was lawful for a long period to order mutilation—the cutting off of a hand or foot or gouging of an eye—as punishment for serious crimes.

No all-embracing legal code existed in Tibet. Only the general moral principles and commandments of Lamaism prevailed. Justice was primarily local and meted out according to custom and usage.

For thirteen centuries, Lhasa was the base of Tibetan politics. The governmental system which evolved was an autocracy, feudal in concept, with the broad structural framework relatively unchanged from the middle of the seventeenth century until modern times. Authority began and pretty much remained at the top, in the executive branch. But to Tibetans, not government but religion was supreme in Lhasa, and the very name of the city, "God's Place," reaffirmed this reality.

For residents and visitors alike, Lhasa embodied the pag-

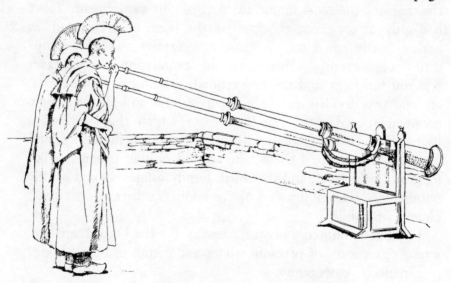

eantry, majesty, fervor and permanency of Tibetan Buddhism. It was a city where the flare of ceremonial trumpets from the top of the white and crimson Potala announced the dawn; where pilgrims not only walked the sacred circle path around the city but fell flat to the ground and measured their way for miles in prostrated lengths; where summer religious festivals prompted merry picnics along the banks of the "Waters of Pleasure"; where the annual changing of residence of the Dalai Lama from the Potala to a summer palace a mile and a half away erupted into a happy holiday procession; where, in short, the usual was unusual.

CHAPTER NINE

The Making of a Monk

IN A Tibetan family at least one son would go off to a monastery while still very young. This was both expected and customary. Since no provision for any system of general schooling existed in Tibet, training for the monkhood offered the only chance for education. It also made it possible for a lay Tibetan of little means to reach a position of respect and eminence.

Probably one out of every six residents of the country entered a monastery. This statistic helps to explain the generally shrinking population. Toward the end of the nineteenth century, an estimated 2,500 cloisters, large and small, housed some 750,000 monks and nuns. Women too went into religious orders but in relatively small numbers. In size alone, the monkhood was staggering in impact.

Monasteries were open to all. Ordinarily a "sponsor" was required, and in the case of a young boy this was usually his parents. But a friend or relative could serve as well. No age limits or academic qualifications were specified. Rich and poor were welcomed equally. Scholars and illiterates both found a

place. Depending on individual ability and inclination, the
student monk could devote himself to learning or give his life
to service in the monastery. The cooking, housekeeping, and
everyday tasks of maintenance represented service areas for
monks. Some simply catered to the community; others obtained
basic vocational training; still others became craftsmen and
calligraphers; a few even emerged as "lama-warriors" or guards.
Motivation of registrants varied; sometimes they ended up at
a monastery because there was no other place to go.

When westerners use the word lama, they generally mean
to imply monk, but in Tibet the title of lama was reserved for
the incarnations of deities and the true spiritual teacher.

Monasteries could be small: just a temple, assembly hall and
living quarters in a remote place. Or they could be a community in themselves, housing up to 10,000 monks and clustering

hundreds of buildings, including auditoriums, dormitories, barns, kitchens, guest apartments, a treasury, altar rooms, and offices. With golden-roofed temples, precious religious ornaments, and the dazzling brightness of their whitewashed facades, some Lhasa monasteries rivaled the Potala in brilliance. The biggest ones, in the vicinity of Lhasa, really were university cities, divided into residences, colleges and faculties.

The daily routine in training for the monkhood tended to be the same, whether in a small monastery or a larger one. Prayer at daybreak, services, psalm-singing, memorization of texts, recitation, tea breaks . . . Let Thubten, now a resident of Switzerland, describe his days in a monastery at Dzongha Dzonz, a small town some 16,000 feet above sea level near Nepal. His parents enrolled him at the monastery before he was seven.

"Our day began before the sun rose, with the ringing of the cloister bells. First, we gathered to pray for two hours, sitting on a long carpet in rows, facing one another, with our legs crossed."

Then it was time for breakfast of butter tea and *tsampa* (a coarse flour made from parched barley). During a free hour, the young monks-to-be arranged and cleaned their living quarters (a cell-like room with a mattress for sitting and sleeping and a low table to be used as a desk), and lit a small fire in a primitive stove to make tea for their teacher. This lama, after drinking his tea, indicated texts to be learned in the coming hours.

"About nine o'clock," continues Thubten, "we all came together again, each with his own book, but we sat apart in separate places. We all spoke aloud in learning our texts. When the main teacher came, he carried a bamboo stick and went quickly to his place. One after another, he called us before him to recite. Anyone who made two or three mistakes was given a blow with the stick by the teacher. The unlucky ones also received an extra text to be learned for the next day."

In the afternoon, the pupils worked at their lessons. Only

at 4 P.M. could they take time out for play and recreation. Before dark they were back in the cloister to take their evening meal. Afterward there was time before they went to bed to repeat the latest memorized prayer lessons.

The general learning levels were pupil, novice, monk on a two-semester system, with less memorizing of scriptures after a sixth class point was reached. Three grades of monks existed: *rapjung*, *getsul* and *gelong*. For *gelong* status, a candidate took the full 253 vows. Ordinarily, studies took 20 to 25 years. They were grouped into main categories of logic, a comparative study of Buddhist scriptures, metaphysics, dialectics, and the Buddhist "truth of the middle way." Candidates were questioned on all these categories at the final examination, which was in the form of a debate. Failures were not so frequent and the occasion brought feasting and gift-giving. From here, the successful monk could proceed to occult studies, including yoga. Tibetans had a special affection for these studies, for which two academies were famous. The most revered lamas became teachers. Or they could choose to practice piety through asceticism to "deliver" all humanity from misery.

The basic literature of Lamaist schools was the *Kangyur*, primarily the direct teachings of Buddha in some 100 volumes of text, plus the Tengyur, more than 200 volumes of commentaries on the *Kangyur*. Tibetans used some visual aids to teaching and meditation; among them were *mandalas* (paintings or diagrams reproducing mystical systems in symbolism of color, line and shape) and *thankas*, (paintings on cloth that served as banners, decoration and meditation pieces). The "Wheel of Life," a spoked disk painted on a scroll, gave vivid pictorial meaning to different forms of existence and the endless cycle of rebirths as seen symbolically.

Within Tibetan Buddhism, there appeared to be a hierarchy by accomplishment and acquirement but also what can be called a "hierarchy by birth." Nearly every monastery in the country housed incarnate lamas or *trülku*, individuals identified as reincarnations of highly revered monks or lamas. Often these descendants from high realms were traced to the original founder of the monastery and served to keep a certain continuity within religious sects. *Trülku* were even graded into four levels. Among "lesser" incarnations, succession was determined by common agreement within a local community, after oracles were consulted, omens followed up, and divine help implored. Methods for searching out *trülku* were somewhat similar to those employed in finding a Dalai Lama but were not so extensive or elaborate. Certainly hundreds of incarnate lamas existed in Tibet, and these were afforded special status. The

THE TIBETAN WIND-HORSE

Tibetan woodcut depicting a good-luck symbol, a "wind-horse" carrying "the flaming jewel"—the triple gem signifying Buddha, the Teachings, and the Monkhood. The surrounding script is made up of mantras—sacred litanies—to invoke good luck and prosperity.

secretariat of the Dalai Lama kept a list of those who had won public recognition. The most eminent was in line to be chosen as a regent to rule during the minority of a Dalai Lama.

Monasteries and their properties were exempt from taxation and so were, in effect, independent overlords. They were self-contained units, administratively, financially and academically. They kept their own property, revenues and riches; exercised a substantial degree of autonomy in curriculum, textbooks and discipline; and discharged all necessary functions of authority within their own boundaries. Every abbot was both political and spiritual leader of his monastery. Every monastery engaged in some trade and commerce as well as in more traditional duties of performing rites for the living and the dead and praying for the welfare of the people. Government endowments included funds and real estate, and private gifts brought in donations of money and goods. Thus monasteries were not only centers of religion and education but self-generating economic units as well. Sometimes the system worked to establish an overburdened, impoverished lower clergy.

The government of Tibet, being a theocracy, invested more power in monks than in laymen. Those schooled in monasteries held the highest positions and exercised supreme secular authority. There was only one instance of a layman filling the office of regent up through 1895. The senior minister of the country's *Kashag* (Council of Ministers) was always a monk. A large proportion of district and other officials were monks. The direct and diffused power of the monkhood was immense. Nationally, the administration of religious affairs was in the hands of a "Head of the Monastic Establishment" and an ecclesiastical department consisting of "chief monk secretaries." These secretaries, popularly known as "the four inside pillars," settled quarrels among lamas, released subsidies to monasteries, and mediated overall questions of general administration. When

TIBETAN HAND PRAYER WHEEL
Contained within the cover are scrolls with OM MANI PADME HUM
inscribed thousands of times.

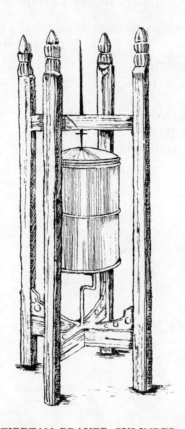

TIBETAN PRAYER CYLINDER

This type of prayer wheel—turned by hand, water or wind—contained cylinders of coiled ribbons on which OM MANI PADME HUM *had been printed thousands of times.*

charged with offenses against the criminal law, monks were tried by monks according to the religious code, not by civil authorities.

Average Tibetans viewed the monkhood as necessary to the whole government, the economy and all religious life. Central religious concern and activity was the realm of monks, lamas and ascetics; ordinary believers depended on members of the monastic community. Believers could and did recite certain prayers and formulas known as "mantras." They turned prayer wheels and invoked, piously and incessantly, their own patron Chenrezi with the most renowned prayer of all, *("Om Mani Padme Hum)*. . . ." They did not hear sermons or make excursions into private prayer. Their appeal, their hope, their trust, their future were packaged in the invocation:

> I seek refuge in the Buddha;
> I seek refuge in the Teachings;
> I seek refuge in the Monkhood;
> I seek refuge in the Teacher of Religion.

CHAPTER TEN

Tibetan Ways of Life

DESPITE invasions and political upheavals, the daily life of Tibetans steadfastly continued in rhythms unchanged for centuries. Even in their strongest period of influence, the Chinese never attempted to redirect these patterns; they were well aware that the people refused to be either distracted or diverted. Devotion to their customs and culture bound Tibetans inextricably together.

For the average resident, life meant herding, farming or trading. Butter tea and *tsampa* provided his basic sustenance. His religious support stemmed from monks, prayers, spirits and propitious offerings. His home was not so poor that it did not have some kind of altar. Families were not so distressed that members could not enjoy singing, games and storytelling. Though theirs was a stern and austere existence, Tibetans did not see it as cheerless or needy.

Within its own borders Tibet produced the staple foods and maintained granary storage reserves against a time of poor crops or famine. From the outside, tea, silk and porcelain were imported from China and items like textiles, rice and sugar from

India. There was no need to import clothing; Tibetans themselves wove the woolen cloth for their distinctive garb. All
incoming supplies were paid for through the wool and skins
Tibetans sold to bring in foreign exchange. No central bank
existed, and barter was widely practiced, though the country
did mint some coins and paper currency. Basically, the country was self-sufficient.

Rich and poor alike wore the traditional *chupa*, a woven
wraparound garment which women wore full-length with a
blouse and a colorful apron and men wore in a pulled-up style
that ended below the knees. A shirt, festively decorated jacket
and sturdy woolen boots completed the men's costume. Minerals and gems found in Tibet, such as gold, silver and turquoise, were fashioned into artistic jewelry for personal
adornment, and even the simplest-living Tibetan seemed able
to afford a ring, for example.

Tibetans often are described as having an innate sense of
good manners and hospitality. It is no surprise that they evolved
a distinct etiquette. Their first step to sociality requires the
presentation of the *khata* or ceremonial scarf. Ordinarily this
scarf is a flimsy, fluffy handful, but when the solemnity of
the occasion demands, it can be twelve feet long and made of
pure silk encrusted with patterns. Tibetans even prescribe the
method of presenting this scarf. In greeting a person clearly
considered superior, the Tibetan raises the *khata* to the height
of his forehead. Shoulder-level giving represents a different
relationship.

At heart Tibetans like to visit, and a considerable amount
of time is spent in welcoming or being welcomed. The traditional refreshment offered a guest is tea, brewed in a little water
to which some soda has been added, then mixed with more
boiling water, salt and butter, and vigorously churned. The
concoction looks creamy, like a soup, tastes rather bitter, and
is endlessly poured into the cup of the visitor. If it is mealtime,
the guest may be served *tsampa* prepared in a variety of ways,

often with cheese; or *moos-moos*, steamed dumplings stuffed with meat; or *phing*, a rice-noodle dish.

The extravagance or frugality of life stemmed from social differences, which certainly existed in Tibet. The monkhood and nobility were privileged classes. From the monkhood sprang the government and the highest religious authority of the land. To this body almost every family contributed at least one member. The nobles, estimated at some 170 families, traced their ancestry to early kings or Dalai Lamas, or in their background was a record of service in government. Laymen did share in the responsibilities of governing and, through their official duties, acquired the status of nobility. Sometimes, too, a rich commoner was deeded the title and the estate of a noble when there were no heirs. Wealthy Tibetans were referred to as "those whose lips are always moistened with tea."

Day-to-day life depended on one's occupation. Nomads, said to represent the "purest" of Tibetans, led the freest kind of existence. There were "independent" nomads and those tending the stock of a wealthy family. They roamed the northern plateau dressed in bulky, raw sheepskins and leading herds of sheep, yak or cattle. They were self-reliant and proud, and rather fierce as they battled the elements as well as marauding wolves and bears.

Sometimes nomad groups were formed consisting of several families related one way or another. They set up a communal home life centered in a large four-sided tent made of yak hair. Then men took the herds to pasture, while the women and children stayed behind, with dogs to guard the tent camp. Within the tent, there were living and cooking areas. Fires were started with flint, and the dung of yak was used for fuel. *Tsampa*, tea, sour milk, dried cheese, soups and meat made up the nomad menu. Tents invariably included an altar with images of Buddha, lamps burning butter, and a few pieces of jewelry. Outside the tent, nomads posted a series of small prayer flags that fluttered in the wind.

During the summer months the nomads moved about in groups from one pasture to another. In the winter they descended from the frigid heights to foothill areas where they could find more shelter and seek out markets to replenish their food stocks. Some nomads never set foot in a Tibetan town during their lifetime. They themselves settled any disputes that arose among them, usually with a "headman" to arbitrate. The common weapon of the nomad, used against animals and thieves, was a sling from which he hurled stones.

These roving Tibetans made their own entertainment by singing, dancing and storytelling. They conducted their own prayers and worship most of the time. But monks did make regular journeys to visit nomad groups and were received with great honor and ceremony. During these visits monks said special prayers, recited scriptures, offered propitious sacrifices, and collected contributions for church festivals.

Farmers were tied to one plot of land, one village, one valley. It was estimated that agriculture engaged five-sixths of the population of modern Tibet. They tilled the land of nobles and landowners, a tract of which was "given" to them in return for services and taxes. Taxes represented a portion of what was produced, and services ranged from soil cultivation to transport work on roads. In this system where work was not paid for directly and property was tied to service, there certainly were possibilities for representatives of authority to demand excessive amounts of both service and taxes. Sometimes a farmer's life was anything but easy.

The farm soil of the country is alluvial, either light brown or grayish in color. It was fertilized traditionally with dung or the fine silt from flood waters. The climate allowed no more than one crop a year. Crops ranged from barley and wheat to turnips and peas. The simplest of farm implements were used, with plows made of wood. Peasants knew some of the rudiments of crop rotation but did not apply them systematically. When grazing lands lay near agricultural areas, the farmer became a combination tiller and stock breeder, pasturing beef and dairy cattle as a sideline.

Small farming villages were spread among fields and meadows. Residents lived in dwellings made of stone and mortar, with one or more rooms which they shared with their farm animals, perhaps a few cows. The villages were self-contained communities. Festivals at harvest time and on religious occasions brought together all the residents, from the wealthiest to the poorest, for rejoicing and feasting. When the harvest was over, peasants took their produce to nearby markets and trading centers to bargain for other needed goods.

At the village level, a "headman" collected taxes and passed them on to the overlord. Usually he was named for a three-year period, but his prestige and influence enabled him to be reelected successively. This job sometimes became hereditary. Beginning at the most elementary level, a strong structure of hierarchy was forged in government which Tibetans took as a matter of course.

Merchants, shopkeepers, traders, artisans and the like made up the middle class of Tibet and were primarily townsfolk. Merchants tended to live quite well, but they did not have the same social status as nobles. Town or city dwellers occupied fairly elaborate houses, usually massive and rectangular, built of stone or oblong sun-dried brick. These consisted of one or more stories, with small windows set not with glass but with paper or cloth for protection. The houses were flat-roofed, with courtyards and wooden balconies, and appeared to be built as sturdily as small forts. A market section or bazaar marked many of the towns—all the bigger ones—and townsfolk and visitors flocked to this section just to look, even if they were not buying and selling.

While private meals for all classes of Tibetans tended to be simple, entertaining could be lavish, with as many as fifteen courses, and livened with special dances, songs and games. For the nobility, this kind of entertainment was frequent. But all people, regardless of their station in life, were expected to offer hospitality to anyone asking for it. There were no hotels and no restaurants to accommodate travelers in Tibet, and in the cities and towns there was a constant flow of traders and pilgrims. Somehow these travelers were always accommodated.

Noble or titled families lived in large town houses and had country estates as well. These dwellings, several stories high, included sitting rooms, bedrooms, prayer rooms, guest rooms, a main kitchen, a tea kitchen, storerooms, a religious assembly hall, quarters for servants, a large courtyard, and huge stables. The life of the nobles had an elegance, affluence and leisure about it, but they could retain their wealth and property only as long as one layman in each generation officially served the government in some responsible position. Their daily life followed the same basic pattern as that of any Tibetan: Rising at an early hour, saying prayers to the gods, drinking tea and nibbling *tsampa* for breakfast, going to occupational duties, eating two meals—one before noon and the other late in the afternoon—then evening prayer and to bed not long after dark. A Chinese scholar of Tibetan life described the Tibetan house as "ill-paved, ill-ventilated, ill-planned and about three-fifths wasted space." To this he might have added "ill-illuminated."

Tibetan families were small because of high infant mortality, a general lack of medical facilities and a considerable incidence of such diseases as smallpox. Concepts of hygiene were not understood, and lavatory facilities—where they existed at all —were most primitive. Only the country's cold, germ-killing climate saved residents from general outbreaks of illness. Medical treatment mostly consisted of herbs and drugs, dieting, bleeding, exorcism and religious rites.

A wide assortment of marital arrangements existed, all geared to keep wealth and property within a family. Monogamy prevailed generally, but polyandry—in the case of the Tibetans, several brothers sharing one wife—became popular. This kept the brothers together as a family and avoided disputes about property. The group amiably shared wife, house and land.

The rich and the titled practiced polygamy sometimes as an expedient means to bind families and clans, or because a first wife proved barren. It was not unusual for a wealthy Tibetan to marry sisters or to take a succession of wives. In another form of marriage a "male bride" married into a family to become its legitimate heir, taking his wife's name, house and fortune. Since there were no sons to carry on the family eminence, it was up to this fortunate gentleman to do so.

Other forms of alliances that seem odd by western standards were completely acceptable in Tibet. Usually there were practical economic reasons. Sometimes a Tibetan married not only his or her mate but all members of the family. To try to trace Tibetan families by blood lines was often virtually impossible because of the strange variety of marital ties.

Western observers have commented on the independent status of Tibetan women compared to that of women in neighboring lands. While the women frequently controlled the family purse strings, could mix freely in social situations and could own property, their role was basically confined to the home. Marriages generally were arranged for them by their families.

Weddings could be extravagant or simple, depending on wealth and social status. But some customs were traditional. A go-between, usually a friend or relative, actually advanced the proposal of marriage, and if it was accepted, the parties involved drew up a contract. This amounted to an engagement, and the dowry was clearly described. The astrologer had already been consulted to confirm that the horoscopes of the young people were in harmony. He also had to determine the most auspicious day for the marriage as well as the exact hour, which could even be before sunrise.

The ceremony itself proceeded with prayers, symbolic food offerings, draping of the *khata*, and ritualistic chants. In a

colorful procession to her new home, the bride wore attached to her back a beribboned arrow decorated in five
different colors to represent five different blessings. This arrow
was an emblem of possession and good fortune. Weddings
were a time of gift-giving and lingering festivities which, in
high Tibetan society, could continue for up to ten days.

Festivals, pageantry and celebrations command unflagging
attention and devotion from Tibetans. Their calendar revolves
around a cycle of festivals, mostly commemorating events in
the Buddhist religion. Though the occasions tend to be solemn
in nature, Tibetans mix in folklore, merrymaking, dance, costume and drama to bestow a joyous exuberance on all holidays.
The New Year's observance is the longest and most elaborate,
with houses decorated, juniper branches burned in special rites
to the gods, puffy, golden-fried pastries called *khabse* prepared,
long hours spent in prayers, and a packed social program of
visiting, feasting, dancing, religious plays and continual toasts
drunk in *chang*. A religious play traditional to the time was the
rousing "Devil's Dance" in which costumed performers de-
picted the punishment of evil spirits by the deities. The height
of action came when a cupful of wine was tossed at the picture
of a demon in a pot of boiling oil, which was then ignited and
shot into the air in flames and smoke. Quite a show, and the
Tibetans loved it.

The fourth month of the Tibetan calendar brings the observances of both Buddha's birth and death. In this "blessed"
month Tibetans accelerate their prayers and good deeds to
accumulate merits toward rebirth, for during this time period
everything—bad and good—is believed multiplied a hundred
thousand times. Penances, pilgrimages, charities and special religious offerings represent the order of each day and the entire
month. Poor and rich alike wend their way toward Lhasa to
make the "holy walk" in a circle which loops around the main
portion of the capital, a total distance of some six miles.

In itself the Tibetan calendar is a distinct feature of the

Tibetan way of life. Months are only numbered instead of having names, and the seven days of the week are named after the sun, the moon and the five visible planets. Each year is identified with an animal combined with an element such as wood, fire, water or iron. For instance, a year can be called Fire-Dog or Earth-Hare or Water-Bird. The calendar works out to a sixty-year cycle, with twelve lunar months in a year but with an extra month thrown in every few years. The state astrologer exercised an original habit of inserting the word *chad* on certain squares of the calendar. These were days foreseen as inauspicious, therefore simply crossed off or cut off the calendar. Then some dates popped up twice, with numbers repeated in consecutive squares to make up for *chads*. Tibetans really never knew what dates would appear on the calendar until a year actually began.

Astrology was extremely vital to Tibetans, and specialists in the art of divination were on call for all important occasions at both the governmental and the personal level. The "auspicious" day in the horoscope would be the only day for a Tibetan to begin a journey, a new effort or new work. A catalog of superstitious beliefs existed. For example, for a person to accidentally spill food on leaving home for a distant place was unlucky. It was a good sign for a sparrow to nest in a house. If one dreamt about a sunrise, this was good, but to dream of a sunset had a bad meaning.

Tibetans never considered life's end as particularly sad. This stemmed from their basic optimism and their conviction of rebirth. Once the "spirit" left the body at death, the principal practical matter that remained was how to dispose of the earthly remains. Sometimes corpses were cremated or buried or—in the case of royalty or high lamas—entombed. The accepted and common method, however, was to feed corpses to the vultures and other birds. The deceased was carried to a mountainside where specialists in the procedure cut up the body, extracted the bones, broke them and ground them into a powder. Then the birds swooped down to do their job. If everything was eaten, it was a good sign. If not, then whatever remained had to be burned or buried.

Brutally jarring to the sensitivities of western visitors, this method of disposing of the dead made sense to Tibetans. It showed their disdain for the human body once it was bereft of the life principle—how little the earthly shell is really worth —and their belief that even in death the body can be useful to other creatures in nature, as a food offering to birds. In a future of countless transmigrations, what reason was there to be overly concerned about a human body?

CHAPTER ELEVEN

Rites, Mysticism and Magic

STORIES of magical happenings are commonplace in Tibet. The people relate tales about monks who have "mastered the wind" and can raise themselves into the air and fly; about saints who live for hundreds of years; about ascetics who can leave their bodies at will and appear to others far away; about oracles who can see far into the future. Impossible feats? Not to the Tibetans, who look upon magic, mysticism, psychic forces and even death as not so mysterious.

The end of physical life, for example, holds no fear for Tibetans. They have a guide to dying called the *Bardo Thödol* (the Tibetan Book of the Dead). This incredible directory tells the deceased how to know his way about *bardo*, a state of "middle being" in which a spirit or soul wanders for forty-nine days before being reincarnated. The whole amazing concept and the specific rites connected with it must be recorded as a great original idea of Tibetans.

A certain group of lamas was supposed to have traveled beyond death and then come back into the material world to inform the living about what to expect in the unknown beyond. Basically, these lamas asserted that life-just-after-death is a dream state in which the soul or spirit often imagines that it still has a physical body, just as humans, in dreams, think they are wide awake and living everyday life. This belief has given rise to a long list of rites in Tibet in which the living make the greatest possible effort to "convince" the dead that they truly are dead. They are firmly told not to come back to their old haunts and are advised to "stop bothering" the living. It is thought that the dying tend to come back when they do not receive the necessary "guidance" at the time of death. A specialized lama called the "Extractor of the Consciousness" is enlisted to help the dying person "liberate" himself from his physical being.

LAMA IN DEMON COSTUME

Only lamas have the right to act in the mystery plays depicting the gods and demons of Tibet.

During the period of "middle being" of the deceased, families prepare certain foods in the room of the departed and carry out different prescribed rituals. A lama recites special scripture to clear the way for reincarnation. It is said that Tibetan houses have low doors and steep stairs so as to prevent a returning spirit—still convinced it is attached to a physical body—from chasing and catching up with the living.

Visitors to Tibet, particularly the early Christian missionaries, were the first to record occult practices too weird and unreal to be believed. One of the early travelers, Abbé Huc, a Lazarist priest who visited the country in the middle 1800s, described a ritual in which a *shaman* (priest) attempted a purification for all the evil around him by offering his own life to purge himself and others. The idea was "to manifest his power; to kill himself, yet not die." Apparently, that was exactly what happened.

The event occurred at an altar raised in front of the temple gate of a monastery before a great gathering of pilgrims. The lama had prepared for the formidable feat with days of fasting and prayer and absolute silence. He seated himself on the altar and placed a large knife on his knees. At his feet a circle of lamas began the invocations and prayers for the ceremony, eventually becoming so excited that they ended up shouting and crying out.

The lama started to tremble in every limb and then went into phrenetic convulsions. Suddenly he threw aside the scarf that enveloped him, seized the knife, and slit his stomach open in one long cut. Blood spurted in every direction, the pilgrims prostrated themselves, and the "victim" was asked about all sorts of future events. His answers were considered oracles.

Calmly now, the recitation of prayers was resumed, and the "sacrificial" lama raised some blood from his wound to his mouth, breathed on it three times and threw it into the air with loud cries. Next he passed his hand quickly over his wound and closed it. All was as before; the "sacrifice" had ended.

Abbé Huc explained in his account that he himself did not

attend the ceremony but gathered the details from various people at the monastery. He concluded there was no "trick" to the operation but that "the devil has a great deal to do with the matter."

This ancient rite was no longer practiced in modern Tibet but certainly the role of oracles was still maintained. Each of the three leading monasteries—Ganden, Sera and Drepung—housed oracles, but that of Drepung, known as Nechung, was considered the most powerful. Nechung rated the title of Chief State Oracle, and the government consulted with him on all important national and international questions. When all major and minor oracles in and near Lhasa gathered every twelfth year, the Nechung oracle was the host. Almost every village in Tibet had an oracle. All acted as mediums, communicating information while in a trance.

One of the best first-hand descriptions of the system was set down by the adventurer and writer Amaury de Riencourt, who visited Tibet in 1947. He witnessed a performance of the Oracle of Gaadong, known for his special power over the weather.

This oracle appeared in a sumptuous robe of white and blue silk brocade, holding a sword covered with jewels, a shining breastplate hanging from his neck. There was strange music and incantations as well as recitations from the holy books as the oracle, half-hidden in darkness on a throne, started exercises to go into a trance. After more than an hour, his face trembled convulsively and the blood appeared to be withdrawing from his face. The fascinated author recorded: "I saw with stupe-faction the bone structure of his face protrude as if it were becoming a death mask, a mere skull covered with thin grey skin."

Then the oracle swayed, struggled, moaned, raged and per-spired and had to be grabbed by restraining attendant lamas, who forcibly seated him. The higher cabinet of Tibet com-municated with him at this time, asking his help in bringing rain because the crops were in danger. Eventually the oracle collapsed and passed out and was carried away. But, yes, the rains did come!

Tibetan yoga encompassed another sphere of seeming magic. An extremely complex art, it requires long study and severe discipline to reach specific goals. There are six different doctrines of this yoga, one of the most astounding being the doctrine of psychic heat, or inner fire. In the achievement known as *tummo*, disciples work at mastering the psychic-nerve system through physical exercises, postures, breathing, meditation and elaborate visualization. If successful, they are able to generate extraordinary body warmth and can live in the most extreme cold wearing only a minimum of clothing.

To test their ability, disciples go out on a cold winter's night to the shore of a river or lake and sit cross-legged and naked on the frozen ground. Sheets are dipped in the icy water, and each neophyte wraps himself in one and must dry it on his body. As soon as the sheet is dry, it is once more dipped in the water and placed on the disciple's body to be dried as before. Sometimes there is competition among disciples as to which can dry the most sheets.

The Tibetans invest even what would seem to be the simplest of church activities—a service consisting mostly of the chanting of prayers—with a kind of hypnotic appeal. Monks and worshippers sit cross-legged on the floor before the sacred altars and begin their worship in a synchronized, flat-sounding round of prayer that soon escalates in tempo, volume and fervor. The chanting has no tonal melody, but the pitch and surge of the sounds and the swaying of the monks caught in the rhythms of the swelling supplications do provoke a mesmerism, a feeling of being caught in some uncanny web.

Everybody prays in Tibet. Even the mountain bandits who make a living by robbing wealthy caravans and traders take time to pray and even build small shrines to the gods near the mountains or hills where spirits are believed to live. The shrines are fashioned from wood, rather like houses without roofs. Inside, the bandits hang prayer flags for protection and luck. Usually these robbers pray before they go out on a sally, and they customarily give a part of what they take to the monasteries. Tibetans do not consider this behavior at all strange, because they believe that very few people are either all good or all bad.

Tibetans like to be assured, through visible signs, that their gods are watching over them and keeping bad spirits away. They carry amulets and portable shrines on their bodies and set up in their rooms family altars to the deities which they keep supplied with cups of water and different offerings of food. They construct prayer walls, temples, *chörten* (pagodas) and monasteries to guard their villages and towns. They twirl prayer beads and prayer wheels and walk around holy places and objects to appease and honor their gods.

Yet Tibetans are conscious, in a very direct way, of things quite invisible, like spirits and demons. These have to be coaxed away by special rites, called "spirit traps," and even exorcism of a symbolic nature. It is common practice, for instance, to try to confuse bad spirits. When a child has been seriously ill in a family, the customary course is to change the name of the youngster. That way the *lha*—spirits that caused the sickness —will not be able to find their victim again.

CHAPTER TWELVE

Independence Under the Thirteenth

FROM 1911 to 1950, Tibet ruled itself in an era of independence. For twenty-one years of this period Thubten Gyatso, the Thirteenth Dalai Lama, led his country through the stormy times of the twentieth century. There were some changes and some measure of modernization, but basically Tibet remained steeped in its past.

To the Thirteenth Dalai Lama fell the task of revitalizing Tibet internally. He too bore the burden of the political destiny of his country in a changing Asia and a changing world. The Thirteenth came to leadership with a first-hand knowledge of two great neighbors, China and India, having spent time in both, and with some understanding of the role of Great Britain in the subcontinent. His record in government set him down in Tibetan history as a highly honored leader: in effect, a modern Great Fifth.

Shortly after assuming political power, the Thirteenth called together the abbots of the large monasteries to advise them to reform their institutions from lax practices and restore a strict discipline. He also acted to decrease the political power of monasteries by appointing more lay government officials. He dealt severely with abuses of privileges within Tibetan society, striking, for example, at the custom of *ulag* whereby government representatives traveling on business could simply requisition horses or yaks for transportation from the local peasants. The Thirteenth saw quite clearly that some officials habitually made unnecessary demands which oppressed the people.

The active reformer moved into many areas. He revised scales of taxation to assess the rich more adequately; revamped the penal system, abolishing capital punishment and all severe sentences involving mutilation except for treason; and introduced a few school reforms. His modernization program extended to reorganizing the Tibetan army, introducing electricity to Lhasa, and stretching telephone and telegraph communication to this city from India in the 1920s. The government even established an English school at Gyantse in 1924, but this was soon closed because some of the high lamas feared its effect on religious beliefs and customs.

As an independent power, Tibet exercised treaty-making rights. A pact was signed with Mongolia in 1913 recognizing the respective governments and sovereignty. In 1914 the important Simla Conference was called to settle questions about the interests of China, Great Britain and Tibet on the Asian continent. Tibet pushed for acknowledgment of its "free" status and acceptance of delineated frontiers with China. The Chinese wanted Tibet proclaimed "an integral part of China" and their "right" to intervention approved.

In compromise, an "Outer" and "Inner" Tibet were devised. The "Outer" region consisted of the area over which the Tibetan government had had jurisdiction for many centuries; the "Inner" represented a politically touchy, broad peripheral area. The autonomy of "Outer" Tibet was recognized, its territorial integrity confirmed, and noninterference in its administration guaranteed. The British secured India's northeast frontier some 800 miles along the crest of the Himalayas from

Bhutan to a meeting place of China, Tibet and the Burmese hinterland in what came to be known as the MacMahon line, having been negotiated by Sir Henry MacMahon. But historically there is some question about the validity of the Simla Convention, because the Chinese only initialed the agreement and the government later disavowed it.

While the Thirteenth Dalai Lama concluded that Tibet should open its door somewhat to the outside world, he also believed this should be done gradually. He welcomed different visitors to Lhasa, among them Americans, British and Japanese. He cultivated closer relations with Great Britain, and in 1921 a British mission visited Lhasa. But the god-king resisted all efforts by foreign powers to exert their influence over Tibetan internal affairs. He strove to maintain Tibet's neutrality in Asian politics and skillfully preserved a balance in her relations with the British in India, the Chinese warlords, and the Soviet Russians, who showed enough interest in Tibet to send a Soviet-Mongol mission to Lhasa in 1927.

The hard-working Thirteenth was rather short, with keen, watchful eyes that protruded a bit, a slightly aquiline nose, large ears, a well-waxed moustache, and what is described as "an inborn noble manner." His day usually began between 5 A.M. and 6 A.M. with prayers for almost two hours, upon the completion of which a monk appeared with a golden teapot to serve the morning tea. Then he busied himself with petitions —mostly asking for his prayers—which he answered directly.

The afternoons were given to political matters. At a cabinet meeting he made judgments on important questions of state. He held audiences for new government appointees and for officials back from tours. During tea ceremony time, between 3 P.M. and 4 P.M., seated on his high official throne and attended by his retinue, he gave audience to those who gathered to worship him. He accepted gifts and blessed the donors by placing his hand on their head.

The Thirteenth Dalai Lama himself best described his life in a political testament of sorts with these words: "After I

took up the duties of spiritual and secular administration, there
was no leisure for me, no time for pleasure. Day and night I
occupied myself with anxious thoughts concerning the problems of religion and state, and deliberated how best I might
promote each of them. . . ."

While his official residence was the Potala, the Thirteenth
normally lived in the so-called "detached" or summer palace
of Norbulingka. He liked to stay there to be closer to nature,
and, being fond of animals, he kept pet horses and the Tibetan
breed of dog called Lhasa Apso.

In internal affairs the Thirteenth Dalai Lama displayed quite
an autocratic manner and would counter no political inter-
ference by the high clergy. Eventually this led to a rift between him and the second highest spiritual authority, the
Panchen Lama. There were indications that the Chinese were
trying to draw the Panchen Lama into their orbit. But the
direct reason for the cold feeling between the leaders and their
followers apparently stemmed from a tax decision. The Tibetan
government decided to tax revenue from the vast estates of the
Panchen Lama—though traditionally they had been exempt—
to raise money for defense purposes. Abruptly, in 1923, the
Panchen Lama fled with his court to China. Apprehension grew
that the Panchen Lama might return to Tibet accompanied by
Chinese military forces. But his exile lasted until his death in
1937.

China, now under Chiang Kai-shek's leadership, began to
show renewed interest in Tibet and in 1930 made overtures
designed to accomplish friendlier relations. During the reign
of the Thirteenth, troubles and clashes with Chinese warlords
in the eastern Kham region had occurred, with both sides
seeking to consolidate positions. These skirmishes almost came
to be considered local conflicts. The Chinese reportedly ad-
mitted they had no control over the warlords of the border,
and the Dalai Lama turned a friendly, listening ear to the
Chinese.

Not long before he died the Thirteenth Dalai Lama made a

startling prophecy. He warned: "Unless we now learn how to protect our land, the Dalai Lama and the Panchen Lama, the Father and the Son, the upholders of the Buddhist faith, the glorious Incarnations, all will go under and disappear and leave not a trace behind. . . ." He predicted that memory of the past would be wiped out; land and property would be taken away from those who held it; a time of famine would come and "all beings will suffer great hardship and pass their days and nights slowly in a reign of terror."

In December 1933 the Dalai Lama "passed out of his Thirteenth Incarnation" at the age of fifty-eight. All Tibet went into mourning. Its face painted with gold, the body of the god-king was embalmed and placed in state in Potala Palace. Thousands of Tibetans came to pay homage and prayed that his spirit would not linger too long in the "Honorable Field" but would reincarnate itself as soon as possible. The people felt a terrible sense of loss and mourned for weeks. Singing, dancing and all merriment was prohibited, and thousands of butter lamps burned on the flat rooftops of Lhasa.

The remarkable Thirteenth left a consolidated and strengthened Tibet, but it was not to remain so. And within two decades his strange prophecy would come true.

CHAPTER THIRTEEN

The End of Freedom

TIBET now entered its final years of freedom. Two regents successively ruled the country from 1933 to 1950. Neither commanded full authority of office or the devoted loyalty of the people that would have unified the nation. Political plots, internal dissension and petty intrigues arose among different religious and secular factions. The course of events clearly pointed up the inherent weakness of the political system. Without a reigning Dalai Lama, the government and administration not only faltered but deteriorated.

Throughout Asia and the Far East, new history was being written. The Communists of Soviet Russia were wooing Outer Mongolia and in 1934 concluded a treaty of alliance. Their influence also was extending to Sinkiang on Tibet's northern border. Nationalist China was digging in for a long war with Japan; the Japanese had launched an attack on Manchuria and then began occupying the entire Chinese coastline. The Chinese government had retreated to Chungkung, uncomfortably close to Tibet.

While these changes swirled in areas not so far away, Tibet

concentrated on its main task: seeking out the child destined to continue the celestial dynasty of the country. An interim ruler was named: Reting Rimpoche, a young incarnate lama with ambition and ability but without any administrative experience. Almost at once this first regency administration faced a difficult situation.

The Chinese dispatched a delegation to Lhasa, ostensibly to convey condolences on the passing of the Thirteenth Dalai Lama. The Tibetans were sure that this mission nourished some political designs as well. The delegation arrived in the spring of 1934, and this foothold led to a mission that lasted until 1949. Members of the mission and Tibetan authorities did discuss various issues, including the continual Chinese-Tibetan border disputes and the return of the Panchen Lama. Tibetans agreed that the Panchen Lama should come back, but without any Chinese military escort. But the Kuomintang regime had its own ideas. This government set him up as their own "Special Commissioner for the Western Regions" and sent him off with 500 armed Chinese soldiers to a point along the Sino-Tibetan border, where he died.

In principle, Tibetans favored resumption of relations with China—but not at the cost of their independence.

The very presence of the Chinese in Lhasa moved the British to send in a mission from India in the summer of 1936. This led to the stationing of a permanent representative in the capital. The Tibetan government viewed this development as a kind of insurance against any mischief being contemplated by the Chinese delegation. The British mission continued until 1947, when India became independent, and the office gradually was converted into a consulate-generalship of the Indian embassy.

In 1940 the Chinese made some presumptuous claims that riled the Tibetans. The sacred, all-important enthronement ceremonies of the Fourteenth Dalai Lama had been set for the first week of the new year—February 22 on the western calendar. The chairman of the Chinese Commission of Mongolian and Tibetan Affairs attended the ceremonies, along with other foreign representatives. Later he asserted that the Chinese had exercised considerable authority in both the selection and enthronement of the new Dalai Lama and that the ceremonies had been, in effect, a Chinese-supervised "show." The Tibetans flatly refuted the outlandish claims.

Earlier, the Tibetan government had been forced to bargain with provincial Chinese authorities for permission to conduct to Lhasa the child identified as the rightful Incarnation. This boy, the son of simple peasants, was found in a far northeast Amdo district in the part of Tibet under Chinese administration. Tibetans requested the area governor to let the child go to Lhasa for further tests. The authorities refused but later relented, provided a ransom was paid. Payment of a sum equivalent to more than $30,000 was demanded. Tibetans raised this amount, but then came further demands, each larger than the last. In all, more than two and a half years elapsed from the time of the first visit of the searching party to the departure of the Dalai Lama's caravan.

All Tibet breathed easier as the four-and-a-half-year-old child was lifted to the golden throne that represented his high office and awesome future responsibility. The "Living God" had returned.

In 1941 the current regent, Reting Rimpoche, unwillingly resigned his position and returned, not too happily, to Reting monastery. As was customary during periods of regency in Tibet, political squabbles, instability and intrigue had been hatched, and the regent had found himself questioned and challenged more and more. An older incarnate lama succeeded to the post, but he was unable to offer the strong, effective leadership that the country needed, especially in the late forties.

Meanwhile, World War II had erupted in Europe, and Tibet attempted to remain quietly neutral. However, when the Japanese invasion of Burma cut off the famous Burma Road and disrupted the overland flow of supplies from the Allied powers to China, Tibet suddenly loomed as an open land-communication route. The Chinese proposed a road to India through the southeastern part of Tibet as an alternate supply route. Despite the urging of the Tibetan government by Great Britain and the United States to accede to this Chinese plan, the answer was negative, at least to the transport of war material. Tibet did agree, eventually, to the transport of goods other than military supplies over its territory.

The whole question caused the government of the United States—which basically had never considered Tibet outside the political framework of China—to take an active interest in the country. In 1942 the Tibetan government granted permission for an American mission dispatched by President Franklin D. Roosevelt to come to Lhasa and from there to proceed to China. The primary object of this mission was to find a new route for supplies from India to China. But the secondary object was to establish the first official contact between the American and Tibetan governments. The members of the mission carried a letter from the American president to the Dalai Lama. They stayed in Lhasa for several months. The idea of an overland supply route proved impractical, and American planes continued to fly the formidable Himalayan "hump" to deliver supplies to China. In January 1944 one of these planes wandered off course, and five crew members bailed out on Tibetan soil before their plane crashed into a mountainside. The airmen found a friendly welcome and assistance from astonished Tibetan villagers. The Americans were also well received in Lhasa, where the unexpected visitors were provided with guides and transport animals to take them to the Indian border.

The American mission pointed up the unofficial but accepted position of Tibet as an independent entity in the eyes of some leading world powers and prompted China to take alarm. Though in the midst of a war for survival against Japan, Generalissimo Chiang Kai-shek pondered how to take action against Tibet. He ordered two warlords in Chinese territory bordering Tibet to invade the country. Fortunately, the independent warlords neglected to carry out the order.

Tibet emerged from the turmoil of World War II unscathed. But internally problems had bubbled. In 1947 a minor civil war broke out in Lhasa. An attempt on the life of Tibet's regent had been made, with the aid of a modern bomb. The episode led to the arrest and mysterious death in prison of the ex-regent, Reting Rimpoche. The ex-regent was accused of being pro-Chinese, and his protégés were dismissed from their posts. Some of these accusations came from a pro-British Young-Tibet group representing a clique favoring British influence. There was no question that Reting Rimpoche had both strong enemies and strong adherents and that his supporters actively wanted him back at the helm in Tibet. The confusing events prompted a serious revolt of monks in the Reting and Sera monasteries against the government. All Lhasa went into a state of alert as the monks and the troops sent to quell the revolt battled. Monks from Sera fled to China, and this strengthened the belief that the Chinese had some part in the attempted coup. According to Chinese accounts, Reting Rimpoche was poisoned in prison.

In foreign relations, the Tibetan government faced a new situation to the south with the emergence of India as a sovereign independent nation and no longer a British dominion. Would the Indian government give Tibet the same diplomatic support received until then from the British in the various difficulties with China? This question caused some anguish until the Indian regime assured Tibet that relations between the two countries would proceed on the same basis as before 1947. However, within a few years India began a policy described by some critics as "the abandonment of Tibet."

Tibetans tried direct international negotiations with the dispatch of goodwill missions to India and China in 1946. Their mission to Nanking did not accomplish much, but it made them aware that the Nationalist government in China was not secure and that the Chinese Communists were making big gains. In 1948 the Tibetan government sent a trade mission to Great Britain and the United States to explore possibilities for direct, expanded trade. Tibet—late, to be sure—was seeking closer ties and friendships with the outside world.

But there was no adequate, forward-thinking political leadership to mobilize the strength of the nation and the support of the world in the trials that loomed ahead for Tibet. The country offered clear evidence of its independence in its customs, currency system, postal arrangements, and civil service. It had made international agreements on its own and was not bound by any treaty or agreement China made with third powers. Chinese visas did not enable foreigners to enter Tibet, but Tibetan passports had validity abroad. Unfortunately, however, no organized world campaign had ever been launched by the Tibetan government to establish the country's independent status as a legal fact, internationally recognized.

In 1949 Tibet made one last grand gesture of independence by ejecting, in July, the whole of the official Chinese mission at Lhasa. The intent was to rid the country entirely of Chinese representation. The mission was without any effective power in Tibet and without any support in China itself, where the People's Republic was soon to be proclaimed by Mao Tse-tung and the Chinese Communists.

As seems completely appropriate to Tibet, the people were forewarned of troubles to come through a series of "supernatural" signs, all indicating bad events ahead. First, a great comet was observed blazing in the sky, and the old-timers related that the last comet seen over Tibet had "heralded" a war with China. Later, without any warning tremors, a violent earthquake struck southern Tibet and caused widespread damage. Other "evil" omens occurred. Babies were born with monstrous defects; a part of a stone column of the Potala was found in fragments; a gilded dragon decorating the Cathedral of Lhasa began to drip water, day after day, though no rain had fallen. Prayers and rites were scheduled around the clock to banish the evil spirits. The people became apprehensive as they awaited the worst. And the worst did come.

CHAPTER FOURTEEN

Invasion and the Aftermath

FROM the very beginning of 1950, signs of the coming storm stalked Tibet. Though the authority of the Nationalist government had been eliminated in China, the new Communist government in Peking complained vigorously about the dismissal of the Kuomintang mission from Lhasa. This action, according to Peking, had been "inspired" by foreign agents in Tibet. The Chinese claim to Tibet was asserted in the strongest terms. But what really alarmed the Tibetans was the proclaimed intention of *chieh-fang* (liberation) of Tibet by this government.

The Peking regime sought to pacify the outside world by declaring that this "liberation" would be by peaceful means. Tibetans, however, believed otherwise. The government appointed delegations to visit India, Nepal, Great Britain and the United States to seek official recognition of the country's independent status, along with some help in keeping out the Chinese. These delegations, however, never left Lhasa because of the negative response from the countries approached. No nation, not even India, wanted to push Tibetan claims against Chinese ones.

Tibetans began to realize they were completely alone in their troubles. The Indian government, still in the process of consolidation itself, was among the first to recognize the new regime in China. It did not want to jeopardize relations with this giant power. Western countries were too far away and too unconcerned to act in any way, and, basically, these nations did not want to presume that China would attack Tibet.

Tibet prepared herself as well as it could. The country's small, ill-equipped and ill-managed army was bolstered with groups of fierce *khambas* from the eastern districts and was reorganized for greater striking power. While individual Tibetans could be hard fighters, they had no real interest in an organized military force. But defense preparations accented training, formation of small mobile units, devising military plans, and stockpiling available weapons and food supplies. At its peak strength, the Tibetan army numbered possibly some 9,000 men. Ammunition and arms were imported from India. Most of the officers were nonmilitary noblemen.

The Tibetans nervously followed Chinese troop and cargo movements into China's so-called Far West bordering on Tibet. In March of 1950 Tatsienlu, located in a buffer district between China and Tibet, was overrun; then local governments, one after another, fell to the Chinese. The "People's Liberation Army" worked at building bridges, improving roads and pushing forward with long convoys of material. More and more border incidents were reported, with Tibetans provoked by Chinese assaults and ambushes.

India advised Tibet to try to negotiate a peaceful settlement with Communist China. In April, a seven-man mission was dispatched from Lhasa to India, where talks could be conducted on "neutral" territory. The Chinese were polite but appeared to have no intention of carrying out serious negotiations.

In May the Peking radio called upon the Dalai Lama and the people of Tibet to submit to "peaceful liberation." The message declared that Tibet was a part of Chinese territory and that the country's geographical remoteness was no obstacle to Communist armies. Peking assured Tibetans that the Chinese would be considerate of their interests and traditions. From Sining a delegation arrived in Lhasa to talk about the Chinese kind of communism, without much success. Tibetan officials were not much interested.

In August the commander of the Chinese Communist Second Field Army flatly announced that forces shortly would enter Tibet to bring the country into the "Motherland's big family," and reinforce China's "line of national defense." Tibet was promised "regional self-government and freedom of religion." From this time onward, sporadic reports erupted in the Indian press and from Hong Kong that the Chinese forces had begun their "liberation."

Basically, the Chinese needed Tibet for strategic and defensive reasons. They wanted to protect their furthest western frontier against possible encroachment. They liked the idea of expanded territory in which they could disperse both their crowded population and new economic theories. They also feared Tibet would become a stronghold of "reactionary" sentiment and of groups not compatible with revolutionary Communist zeal. Having shaken off a corrupt and unpopular government in their own country, the Chinese expected Tibetans to welcome change and "progress." But the reaction of Tibet was something quite different.

While the Tibetan mission to India continued its pursuit of negotiation with the Chinese; while the Chinese ambassador in India assured officials there that his country endorsed peaceful intentions; while the attention of Asia and the western world was riveted on another trouble spot—Korea—the fateful blow to Tibet was dealt. The Chinese Communists invaded. The date: October 7, 1950. The "liberation" was begun.

News of the invasion was slow in reaching the outside world, and reports emerged confused and garbled. Asian and western nations seemed unprepared to believe that a large-scale attack had been launched. Even in India, only a fragmented version of what had happened was circulated at first. Mostly, the

immediate accounts came by way of yak drivers and mule-
teers who dispensed information at India's gateway to Tibet.
One report said that the Chinese, using wiles, had set off
hundreds of rounds of rockets, star wheels and other fireworks
to threaten and to scare into surrender the Tibetan soldiers
stationed at Chamdo in eastern Tibet. It was the Kham district
that fell first, reportedly on October 19. Only on October 24
did the Chinese themselves announce: "Units of the Chinese
People's Army have been ordered to cross over into Tibet to
liberate three million Tibetans from imperialist aggression, to
complete the unification of the whole of China, and to safe-
guard the frontier regions of the country."

The Chinese stormed Tibet with some 40,000 soldiers, at-
tacking simultaneously at several points along the eastern
frontier but sending in as well a smaller force that entered the
uplands of northwest Tibet. The attack was both bold and
elaborately organized. After the invaders had wiped out
Tibetan frontier garrisons in Kham, the army converged from
at least five directions on Chamdo, a strategic point where a
large contingent of Tibetan forces were concentrated. The
vastly superior weapons and organization of the Chinese, along
with their overwhelming number of soldiers, overcame Tibetan
resistance. During the retreat of the Tibetans, the fiercely
fighting Khamba warriors held off the Chinese to allow the
government troops to withdraw. Apparently there were communication problems between Chamdo and Lhasa, for it was
only on October 28 that Lhasa officially confirmed that Chinese
troops had entered Tibet from the east. By then the Chinese
were consolidating their position and calling on captured provincial officials to help shape a national peace.

Even after the assault began, the optimistic Tibetans hoped
to find some formula for appeasing the Chinese while yet keeping some semblance of independence for their country. Also,
there was at least a small group of nationals in eastern Tibet
who dissented from Lhasa policies and programs and opposed
neither the invasion nor the Chinese. Also, some Tibetans

clung to the thinking of past centuries that a "priest-patron" relationship could be restored. The folly of this belief soon was seen.

The Tibetan government requested Indian diplomatic assistance in the dispute. In response, India sent the Chinese government a note expressing "surprise and regret" at developments in Tibet. The Chinese firmly replied that Tibet was "an integral part of Chinese territory" and that the matter was "entirely a domestic problem of China." Clearly, Communist China believed it possessed "sovereign rights" in Tibet.

To whom could Tibet now appeal? The beleaguered land turned to the United Nations. It charged China with aggression and noted in its appeal that ". . . the Chinese revolution in 1911 which dethroned the last Manchurian emperor snapped the last bonds that Tibet had with China. Tibet thereafter depended entirely on her isolation, her faith in the wisdom of Lord Buddha, and occasionally on the support of the British in India for her protection. . . ." Not being a member of the UN, Tibet searched hard for a sponsor to introduce its resolution, finally finding a friend in tiny El Salvador. But the General Assembly voted not to consider the question of Tibet —mostly because the big powers wanted to avoid any clash with China—so the matter was shelved for nine years! Even when resurrected, the whole question was watered down to a very slight objection. The Tibetan request for a UN commission to visit Tibet to get the facts was ignored.

Meanwhile, the people of Tibet took renewed hope from the installation of Tenzin Gyatso as the Fourteenth Dalai Lama at a minority age of fifteen. On November 17, 1950, full ruling power was transferred to him, and the Chinese problem came under his authority. Though not yet of age, the Dalai Lama accepted the responsibility at the urging of the cabinet and the pronouncements of the oracles. When the famous State Oracle was consulted, he fell down before the Dalai Lama in a trance, shouting: "Make him king!" There was, in truth, no other course.

About a month after taking office, the Dalai Lama shifted his government to Yatung, close to the Sikkim border, to be out of personal danger in the event of an attack on Lhasa and to be in a position to seek asylum in India should this prove necessary. Before he left he took tea with his officials, and his empty cup remained on the low table where he set it as a sign that he would return. With the young Dalai Lama at the border, Tibet had some bargaining power with the Chinese, who knew that if he crossed the border, he would take the government and the heart of the people with him.

Under this arrangement, Tibet proceeded with "peace" negotiations, dispatching representatives to Peking. With no help coming from any land, the Tibetans had to come to terms with the invader.

Those terms were harsh. Under an agreement concluded in Peking in May 1951, Tibet became a part of China, with provisions spelling out the military domination of the country by the Chinese Communists. The seventeen-point agreement, however, did specify autonomy for Tibetans in internal matters and a policy of noninterference in religious beliefs, customs and traditions. Tibetans viewed these concessions as "honey offered on a sharp knife" and wondered about their practical reality. Basically, the agreement appeared to effect the transformation of Tibet into a military district of China.

The Dalai Lama moved back to Lhasa at about the same time as a Chinese administrator sent from Peking established himself in the capital. This administrator was soon joined by a variety of assistants who made it a custom to arrive in the escort of thousands of soldiers. In less than a year, some 10,000 Chinese had descended upon Lhasa alone, causing housing difficulties, food shortages, and bitter complaints from residents. The military occupation of the country fanned out from eastern Tibet, where the Chinese had completed a network of transport and supply lines.

At first the occupiers tried not to offend Tibetans, behaving in a reasonable manner. They sought to win minds through their propaganda, and popularity through farming improvements, use of mechanized vehicles and other "novelties". While Tibetans are curious by nature, they also are traditionally strong in their beliefs. They balked at attempts to change their way of thinking and resented imposed patterns that tended to destroy customs that set them apart. Tension and discontent inevitably cropped up between the resentful Tibetans and the uninvited Chinese.

Chinese military and civil officials found reforming Tibet to be almost impossible. In 1952 they moved to make inroads on the authority of the Dalai Lama. They called for the dismissal of two chief ministers and divided the country into three administrative zones so as to reduce the power of the Dalai Lama. To counteract the god-king, they built up the importance and power of the Panchen Lama, who by custom had no political significance. This Panchen Lama was considered a bogus incarnation, because he had been "discovered" and chosen in China and brought up entirely under Chinese control. The Peking regime returned him to Tibet to head the government of western Tibet. The people called him "Mao's Panchen," yet gave him the respect due his position. In the end, this Panchen proved that he was not a political puppet, and he had to be deposed by Chinese authorities.

In 1954 the Dalai Lama was invited to visit China, and his departure caused a terrible surge of anguish in the country. There were fears for his personal safety. The Chinese nourished some hope that Tibetans would come to regard their ruler as a kind of government worker in the Tibetan region of China. But the rapturous mass demonstration with which the people greeted the Dalai Lama upon his return from China some six months later clearly showed the Chinese that he was regarded as their one true leader.

Resistance to Chinese rule was growing. A *mimang* ("people's group") had been formed which began to take some organized political and guerrilla action against the occupiers. Monks and monasteries rallied to the call for some active defense. Revolts first broke out in eastern Tibet, the area longest under Chinese domination. Here China's policy of collective farming had resulted in large-scale immigration and colonization, and Tibetans faced the eventuality of being "absorbed" on their own soil. The Chinese announced a program of settlement that would bring in two Chinese colonists for every Tibetan resident. Tibetans saw, all too starkly, what would happen to their culture, beliefs and practices.

Armed resistance was sporadic and stemmed in different places from different causes. The list of causes lengthened: Tibetans chafed under youth indocrination, "requisitioning" of labor and food supplies, new taxation, disrespect for religious practices and institutions, deportation of the male population, sending children to China for training, and replacement of popular Tibetan officials with Communist sympathizers. The increasing outbreaks of fighting prompted the Chinese to undertake military operations with armored vehicles and aircraft. All weapons held in monasteries or by individuals were taken by force. Punitive expeditions by the occupiers to the areas of greatest unrest caused Tibetan casualties to mount. Guerrilla bands were formed to fight back and to disrupt enemy convoys. Traffic through the Kham region on the Chamdo-Lhasa road became so dangerous that Chinese drivers called it the road of death.

A general uprising was in the making, with the organization of fighter units throughout the country. But Lhasans were not allowed to participate in military aspects of any uprising because of fears that damage could be inflicted on the Holy City and retaliation taken against the Dalai Lama. The resistance had no illusions about defeating the Chinese; the idea was to attract some attention and possibly help from the outside world. Unfortunately, not much about the active unrest in Tibet reached the outside world, though some reports about Tibetan resistance and sabotage against the Chinese began to circulate in India. Also, an increasing number of Tibetans escaped over the border on the pretext of making pilgrimages to India.

In December 1956 the Dalai Lama, along with the Panchen Lama, went to India to observe the 2500th anniversary of Buddhism. The Chinese advised the Dalai Lama to stay in Lhasa, but he chose not to take this advice. While in India the Dalai Lama traveled widely, conferred with different leaders, talked with the visiting Chinese premier, Chou En-lai, and debated whether he should return to Tibet at all. The Chinese relented somewhat and promised some concessions to the Tibetans. The Dalai Lama asked for removal of Chinese troops, restoration of the Dalai Lama's previous status, reinstatement of ministers dismissed, and abandonment of the Chinese "reform" policy. The Chinese agreed to a limited withdrawal of troops and political cadres and announced that "reform" for Tibet would be postponed at least five years.

Early in 1957 the Dalai Lama returned to Lhasa. The Chinese began some of the changes they had agreed to make, but these were short-lived. New harassments and repressive actions occurred, and the whole posture of the people stiffened. A proposed visit of India's Prime Minister Jawaharlal Nehru in 1958 was cancelled at the insistence of the Peking regime. The ever-swirling storm in Tibet had yet to reach its climax, a climax that would send the god-king on a dramatic journey that shocked and aroused the outside world to the plight of a lost corner of the globe.

CHAPTER FIFTEEN

The God - King Chooses Exile

IN FEBRUARY 1959 Lhasa teemed with huge crowds spilling into the capital for the New Year's festivities. In the face of religious and cultural repression, Tibetans continued their traditions with more and more fervor. The Year of the Earth Pig, however, was almost dreaded rather than welcomed. Tension, conflict, and anxiety gripped the entire land. The people shuddered at the thought of what the future could bring. They seemed to sense the approach of some dramatic emotional turning point.

Tibetans saw clearly that the Chinese could not and would not accept the traditions and history of a land ruled and influenced by lamas. Monks were being forced into secular life and work; the power of the Dalai Lama was being whittled away, with a so-called Preparatory Committee taking over administration of the country; the resources of Tibet in grain reserves and previous metals were being depleted; the general population was being conscripted for forced labor to build roads and for other projects; villagers were being dispossessed and large estates confiscated, with Chinese settlers arriving to take over the land.

Early in March, elements of a new Chinese army division arrived in the capital, and sporadic riots erupted. The occupiers had become so unbearable in eastern Tibet that about 10,000 refugees from Kham and Amdo had drifted into the Lhasa area, causing additional crowding, confusion and food shortages. When the rumor spread that the Chinese intended to abduct the Dalai Lama to Peking, the capital became a tinderbox, waiting for a spark to touch it off.

That spark flamed in a report being circulated that the Chinese had asked the Dalai Lama to attend, without his usual guards, a cultural show at the Chinese military headquarters, with the date fixed for March 10. Whether true or not, the people jumped to the conclusion that the stipulation that he appear without guards meant that the Chinese were about to kidnap their god-king. Spontaneously, thousands of residents and rebels from other areas moved into the streets of the city in a spontaneous demonstration, with a substantial contingent of women among them. The moving mass surrounded the Norbulingka residence of the Dalai Lama to keep him there and to prevent the Chinese from reaching him. The god-king did not stir from the palace, and the whole episode angered the Chinese.

The milling Tibetans—estimated at some 30,000 at least—remained in the streets to form a mass bodyguard for the Dalai Lama. They continued to fear that some attempt would be made to take him away. There were clashes, some firing and fighting, and rebellious chanting about a return of independence for Tibet. The Chinese moved more troops—variously estimated from 30,000 to 70,000—closer to Lhasa, and heavy guns encircled the city.

The besieged Dalai Lama consulted with his monk and lay advisers as to the future. The possibilities were limited. All-out open rebellion by the Tibetans could not reasonably be pur-

sued; a revolution would be crushed immediately in the face
of the superior arms and forces of the Chinese. Further "co-
operation" with the occupiers? The Dalai Lama had worked
with patience and persistence to preserve the integrity of the
country's traditions and administration while somehow keeping
peace with the Chinese. Yet this course had not benefited the
nation. Flight to some nearby sanctuary? More than any other
person or symbol, the Dalai Lama had rallied, supported and
sustained the people because he was, after all, not just a leader
but a god-king. In him Tibet—past, present and future—
existed. "I shall go," proclaimed the Dalai Lama, "if by going,
I can help my people and not merely save my life."

No less than his previous incarnations, this lean, sensitive
Fourteenth Dalai Lama was bestowed with titles of highest
esteem—"Precious Protector," "The Presence," "Wishful-
filling Gem"—and with the awesome trust of the nation. The
destiny of Tibet, in the most critical period in the entire history
of the country, rested in his hands.

The twenty-four-year-old god-king reflected, consulted,
prayed, and listened to the oracles. The final argument for the
most critical decision this Dalai Lama ever had to make came,
finally, from the outside. On March 17 Chinese troops fired
mortar shells at the summer palace, two of which fell on the
grounds. Whether they were fired as a warning, a scare
technique, or a gesture of strength is unknown. The incident
was interpreted as menacing the very person of the Dalai
Lama. If additional support for a plan of flight was needed,
this was it. The Dalai Lama bowed to a fateful decision.

That very day the plan for the great escape was set into
motion. Preparations for such an eventuality had been made.
Food was stocked; a part of the fabulous treasure at the command of the Dalai Lama was packed for transport by mules;
members of the Dalai Lama's family, his close advisers and
ministers were alerted to be ready for flight.

Senior government officials in the escape party began leaving Norbulingka palace in small groups. It was still a time of

traditional festivity, and visits by Lhasa's officials to one another did not cause suspicion among the Chinese. These officials unobtrusively made their way to an agreed meeting place south of Lhasa. The Dalai Lama's mother, sister and younger brother left the capital and, unnoticed, proceeded to the same point by a different route.

At the critical moment the Dalai Lama left his palace, removed his glasses, disguised himself as a member of his own bodyguard, and took with him as an article of identification the insignia of his high office, the famous Red Seal which only the Dalai Lama is permitted to use. Some accounts of the escape relate that the Dalai Lama was dressed in monk's robes. But the Fourteenth god-king relates in his autobiography, "My Land and My People": "A soldier's clothes and a fur cap were left for me; I put them on."

With other guards, he started on a routine inspection tour, mingling with the crowds still in the area. Under cover of nightfall, the Dalai Lama made his way to a point along the banks of the Kyichu. He successfully eluded Chinese patrols guarding exits from and entrances to the city. He did not cross the river at the usual ferry point; he was conveyed by boat for some miles to a location where Khampa guerrillas waited to escort him further. From here the Dalai Lama, now well protected, advanced to join members of his family and other escapees.

The flight route from that point on was subject to change. "Runners" for the Khampa resistance movement kept the party posted on the positions of the Chinese on possible routes ahead. Apparently it was hoped that the Dalai Lama and his group could proceed along main routes to Bhutan, but the presence of many Chinese patrols ruled out this plan. A difficult caravan route, familiar to Tibetans, was quickly decided upon as the most feasible.

The party crossed the Tsangpo River in small groups on yak-skin rafts. Once across this wide and turbulent waterway, the group made for Minden-Ling, a resistance center some thirty miles away. Fresh horses awaited the travelers at different stops, and Tibetan fighter units appeared as escorts. A large group of fighters were left behind to cover the escape route.

Traveling a route of some 200 miles through southern Tibet that led to the frontier town of Tsona Dzong, the party crossed treacherous mountain terrain, rivers, valleys and snow-covered passes. Sometimes the group trekked up to twenty miles a day, sometimes much less in crossing passes at 18,000 feet altitude. There were steep climbs and sudden descents, occasionally on small and narrow ledges with high rocky walls on the sides and perilous chasms below. The escape took fifteen days, with the group moving as a caravan, and since the group followed a route where caravans were frequent, it was difficult for the Chinese to spot the Dalai Lama and his party. Some extra precautions were taken to avoid detection. The group tried to keep to the shelter of trees and shadowing rock formations by day and did considerable traveling by night. When time came to rest, the party set up yak tents or stayed in peasant huts. Once, at least, a plane droned overhead and the group scattered, but the aircraft flew on.

Two days after the Dalai Lama slipped out of the palace, the Chinese became aware of his departure. A bombardment of Lhasa began, with severe shelling of Norbulingka. The Chinese accused Tibetan guerrillas of "abducting" the Dalai Lama, and punitive action was demanded. The simmering spark of rebellion in Lhasa flamed into a fierce general uprising—a hopeless battle from the start but one which the people and the resistance fighters launched in fury and desperation. It took the Chinese five days to put down the uprising; widespread damage was done to Lhasa and its nearby monasteries, and a military control committee was set up in the capital. The Chinese tersely proclaimed: "At present, Tibetan autonomy and military control by the Chinese People's Liberation Army are simultaneously in force." Thousands of Tibetans lost their lives or were taken prisoner. The outside world acknowledged that not reform but rebellion had gripped the Roof of the World.

The Chinese quickly ordered pursuit of the Dalai Lama, but the task proved difficult because the escape route was not known. All their detachments at border points were put on alert. The Chinese realized that they could neither injure nor kill the god-king, because such unspeakable action would turn the entire nation against them in wrath. It is quite possible that the Chinese spotted the caravan of the Dalai Lama but found themselves in the position of being able to do nothing. Only they could answer the question of whether they had gained or lost with the flight of the Dalai Lama.

Meanwhile, the Dalai Lama and his party continued their suspenseful journey at top possible speed, for once they reached Tsona Dzong the threat of any intervention or attack would virtually vanish. This last lap was a strenuous fifty-mile stretch through high mountains. At last, on March 31, a weary party of eighty travelers—the Dalai Lama, his family, cabinet members, senior government officials, tutors, attendants and protectors—crossed into Indian territory at the Chutangmu pass to reach the tiny town of Tawang.

As he approached the Indian border, it is reported that the Dalai Lama dismounted from his horse and stood silently looking back at the stark mountainous face of his native land. He remained in quiet thought and meditation as the monks who accompanied him chanted hymns and all members of the party paused for their own interlude of farewell. The reflections of the Dalai Lama at this emotional moment were completely his own.

But certain circumstances and signs of the future could be clearly read. The Dalai Lama knew that as "The Chosen One" he would continue to be the religious and temporal head of Tibet as long as he lived and wherever he lived. In the Tibetan way of thinking, this was a fundamental concept. It meant that he could not relinquish the effort and struggle to help his country and his people in their determined, stubborn fight for preservation. He carried with him the burden, the crisis and the fate of Tibet, yet most importantly he remained the receptacle of hope for all his countrymen.

(Was there a future for Tibet? All present indications were bleak: bitterness, repression, destruction, violence, unwelcomed change, transgression of human and civil rights, and imposition of a new pattern of culture.)The response of the people—in outright resistance, secret sabotage and passive non-cooperation—seemed sure to continue in one part of the country or another. What the Dalai Lama might not have anticipated was the action of Tibetans in following his example, choosing to live as refugees. Close to 80,000 residents were to flee Tibet, crowding into Asia and dispersing to many western countries on the face of the globe, particularly neutral Alpine Switzerland. These thousands could not claim a land of their own, but they could claim a leader, their own Dalai Lama. They could try, in a tolerant foreign setting, to sustain and maintain their very individual culture and religion.

When the Dalai Lama crossed the border from Tibet into the sanctuary of India, he made modern history and a solemn, saddening personal decision. He had chosen the lonely life of exile.

FROM "annexed" Tibet, only sporadic reports now reach the outer world. No real contact exists between the thousands who have fled and those who have remained. The former church-state has been "reformed" to proletariat political and social patterns of Chinese communism. The "Roof of the World" as an independent area has been erased from the maps.

But Tibet as a people and civilization still survive. Within the country, the people cling as they can to their own customs and manners. Outside the country, refugee Tibetans scattered in the east and west have carried their beliefs and legacy with them. *Om Mani Padme Hum* resounds in odd corners; chupa-garbed residents scurry along in sophisticated world capitals; carved Buddha hand altars and portraits of the Dalai Lama decorate contemporary living rooms, and the *khata* is proffered in gratitude to hosts in many lands. Even the wind gives testimony to those places where Tibetans have gathered in numbers, for, strung above their dwellings, small cloth "prayer flags" flap in the breezes.

Will transplanted Tibetans forget what is uniquely their heritage in the necessary, and sometimes trying, adjustment to living in new lands? "Temporarily, we may," comes a realistic answer from a Tibetan now rooted in Switzerland. "But what truly lives within us cannot be lost."

For Tibetans and those outsiders who had opportunity to know it, "Old" Tibet represents a singular kind of treasure. These voices proclaim that, where this treasure lies, there too lies the heart, the unfolding lotus, the symbol of spiritual development. Just as the lotus flower lifts itself through muddy waters to blossom exultingly above the surface, so too has "Old" Tibet grown beyond the mortal earth, to remain triumphant in unearthly blossom.

Bibliograpy

Barber, Noel. *From the Land of Lost Content: The Dalai Lama's Fight for Tibet*. Boston, 1970.

Bell, Sir Charles. *Tibet: Past and Present*. Oxford, 1924.

_____. *The People of Tibet*. Oxford, 1928.

_____. *The Religion of Tibet*. Oxford, 1931.

Bernard, Theos. *Land of a Thousand Buddhas*. London, 1952.

Bureau of the Dalai Lama. *Tibetans in Exile: 1959-1969*. Dharamsala, 1969.

Clarke, Sir Humphrey. *The Message of Milarepa*. London, 1958.

Dakpa, Rinchen and Rooke, B.A. *In Haste from Tibet*, London, 1971.

Dalai Lama the Fourteenth. *My Land and My People*. New York, 1962.

Das, Sarat Chandra. *Contributions on the Religion and History of Tibet*. New Delhi, 1970.

David-Neel, Alexandra. *Initiations and Initiates in Tibet*. London, 1931.

De Riencourt, Amaury. *Lost World: Tibet, Key to Asia*. London, 1950.

Ekvall, Robert B. *Religious Observances in Tibet: Patterns and Functions*. Chicago, 1964.

Evans-Wentz, W. Y. *Tibetan Yoga and Secret Doctrines*. London, 1935.

_____. *The Tibetan Book of the Dead*. London, 1927.

_____, ed. *Tibet's Great Yogi Milarepa*. London, 1928.

Ford, Robert. *Wind Between the Worlds*. New York, 1957.

Govinda, Lama Anagarika. *Foundations of Tibetan Mysticism*. London, 1960.

Grenard, F. *Tibet: The Country and Its Inhabitants*. London, 1904.

Harrer, Heinrich. *Seven Years in Tibet*. London, 1953.

Hutheesing, Raja, ed. *Tibet Fights for Freedom*. Bombay, 1960.

Kolmas, Josef. *Tibet and Imperial China*. Canberra, 1967.

Li, Tish-Tsang. *Tibet: Today and Yesterday*. New York, 1960.

MacGregor, John. *Tibet: A Chronicle of Exploration.* New York, 1970.

Moraes, Frank. *The Revolt in Tibet.* New York, 1960.

Norbu, Thubten Jigme and Turnbull, Colin M. *Tibet, Its History, Religion and People.* London, 1968.

————, as told to Heinrich Harrer. *Tibet Is My Country,* London, 1960.

Patterson, George. *Tibet in Revolt.* London, 1960.

Rahul, Ram. *The Government and Politics of Tibet.* New Delhi, 1969.

Richardson, H. E. *A Short History of Tibet.* New York, 1962.

Shakabpa, W. D. *Tibet: A Political History.* New Haven, 1967.

Shen, Tsung-lien and Liu, Shen-chi. *Tibet and the Tibetans.* Stanford, 1953.

Sinha, N. Chandra. *Tibet: Considerations on Inner Asian History.* Calcutta, 1967.

Snellgrove, David and Richardson, Hugh. *A Cultural History of Tibet.* New York, 1968.

Stein, R. A. *Tibetan Civilization.* London, 1972.

Tada, Tokan. *The Thirteenth Dalai Lama.* Tokyo, 1965.

Taring, Richen Dolma. *Daughter of Tibet.* London, 1970.

Thomas, Lowell, Jr. *Out of This World: Across the Himalayas to Forbidden Tibet.* New York, 1950.

————. *The Silent War in Tibet.* New York, 1959.

Tucci, Guiseppi. *Tibet: Land of Snows.* London, 1967.

Waddell, L. A. *The Buddhism of Tibet, or Lamaism.* Cambridge, 1934.

Index

Ambans, 51-52
Amdo, 11, 96, 111
Anthropology, 7
Area, 6-7, 50-51
Astrology, 81
Atisha, Pandit, 21-22

Bardo Thödol (Book of the Dead), 83. *See also* Death rites
Bell, Sir Charles, 1
Bod, 10-11. *See also* Origin of Tibet
Bön, 18, 19, 27, 37
Buddhism; early appearance, 18-19; early persecution, 20-21; "New Spread," 21-22; Mahayana, 26-27, 29;

Tibetan Buddhism, *see* Lama and Lamaism

Calendar, 80-81
Chamdo, 7, 11, 104, 108
Chang tang, 5, 9, 10
Chao Erh-Feng, 55-56
Chenrezi, 1, 8, 16, 18, 39, 42, 71
Chiang Kai-shek, 92, 97-98
China (and Tibet): early relations, 17-18; treaty of A.D. 821, 20; under Mongol Asian supremacy, 29-30, 31-32; under the Manchus, 40, 44, 50-54; Peking convention, 55; relations with Nationalist China, 92, 97-98; with Commu-

nist China, 101-103; invasion and consolidation, 103-106; Tibetan resistance, 107-108, 111-112, 116; Communist occupation and 'reforms,' 110-111, 116. *See also* Dynasties (China) and Treaties
Chou En-lai, 109
Cities (main), 11. *See* Lhasa
Civil strife, 30, 36, 51-52, 96, 98
Curzon (George Nathaniel), 53

Dalai Lama (god-king), 2, 12; rise of, 35-37; derivation of title, 37-38; system of 'discovery,' 39-41; beliefs about, 36, 39, 42, 112; enthronement and training, 41-42, 96; overall role, 34, 36, 38, 42, 115-116; earliest, 35-38. *See also* separate listings for Fifth, Sixth, Seventh, Thirteenth and Fourteenth Dalai Lamas
de Riencourt, Amaury, 86
Death rites, 81-82, 93
Desideri, Ippolito, 47
Dorjiev, Agvan, 54
Dress (traditional), 74
Dsungars, 49, 51
Dynasties (China): Tang, 17; Ming, 31, 33, 38;

Ching, 44; Manchu, 38, 44, 49, 50-51, 53-54, 56

Economy, 9, 10, 73, 74, 108, 116
Electricity (introduction to Lhasa), 90
Exiles (Tibetan), 108-109, 116

Farms and farming, 76-77, 108
Festivals, 45, 80, 110
Fifth Dalai Lama: achievements, 43-46; 'retirement' and death, 47
Foods, 73, 74, 75
Fourteenth Dalai Lama: 'discovery,' 95-96; installation, 105; journey to India, 109; besieged, 111-112; flight into exile, 112-115

Gedun Truppa (First Dalai Lama), 35, 36
Gelupka (Yellow Hat) sect, 32-34, 36, 37, 38
Genghis Khan, 30
Geography, 5-7
'Golden Age,' 20
Government, 11-12; under kings, 17, 20-21; under religious hierarchies, 29, 34, 43-45; under the Manchus, 50-53; under the

'Modern Fifth,' 89-91; under Communist China, 106-107, 109. *See also* Dalai Lama

Great Britain and Tibet, 52-54, 89, 90, 91, 99, 101, 105

Gurkhas, 52

Gushi Khan, 38, 44

Gyalwa Rimpoche: *See* Dalai Lama

Gyantse, 11, 55, 90

Health, 78

Himalayas, 2, 5, 6, 15, 52, 90

Homes and communities, 75, 77, 78

Hospitality, 74, 77, 78

Huc, Abbé, 85-86

Incarnate Lamas (trülku), 27, 67, 68

India and Tibet, 15, 18-19, 46, 50, 53, 55, 89, 90-91, 95, 101-102, 109, 115-116

Isolationism, 1-2, 3, 50, 52-53, 91, 98-99

Jokhang (cathedral), 58-59

Kangyur, 67

Karmapa (sect), 33, 36

Kashag, 12, 61, 70

Kashmir, 6

Khan, Altan, 37, 38

Khan, Kublai, 30

Khata (ceremonial scarf), 74, 79

Kings: early legendary, 15; first historical, 16-17; other, 20-21; 'lay' kings, 31, 36, 51

Kyichu (river), 57, 59, 113

Lama and lamaism, 27-28, 31, 64-71

Land (ownership), 12-13, 76

Lang Darma, 20-21

Language, 18

Law, 62, 90

Lha (spirits), 19, 88

Lhasa, 11, 18, 46, 50, 51, 56, 57-62, 91, 95, 97, 109, 110

Lhato Thori, 16

Legends, 7-8, 21

MacMahon line, 90-91

Mao Tse-tung, 99

Marpa, 25

Marriage (customs), 78, 79, 80

Milarepa, 22, 23-28

Minerals, 10

Missionaries, 47

Monasteries: Ganden, 32, 86; Drepung, 33, 46, 86; Sera, 33, 86, 98; Tashi Lhunpo, 35; Reting, 98

Mongols, 29, 30, 31, 37, 49

Mönlam (festival), 45, 110

Mount Everest, 5

Nirvana (final bliss), 27, 36
Nomads, 75-76
Norbulingka, 92, 111, 112, 114
Nyingmapa (sect), 33

Om Mani Padme Hum (prayer), 16, 71-72, 116
Oracles, 40, 86-87, 112
Origin of Tibet, 10-11

Padmasambhava, 19
Panchen Rimpoche, 35, 44, 92, 93, 94, 95, 107, 109
Pandit, Atisha, 21-22
Peking, 44, 49, 55, 56, 106
Phakpa (the Saint), 30
Population, 6-7, 104
Potala, 18, 46, 59, 60, 61, 63

Ralpachen, 19, 20
Regents, 12, 47, 61, 94, 96, 98
Regions, 11
Religion: See Buddhism; also Lama and lamaism
Reting Rimpoche, 95, 96, 98
Richardson, H. E., 51
Rivers, 9, 10, 51, 57
Rockhill, W. W., 44
Russia and Tibet, 54, 55, 91, 94

Sakya (sect), 29, 30, 31
Seventh Dalai Lama, 50, 51

'Shaman,' 19, 85
Shigatse, 11, 29, 36
Sikkim, 53, 55
Simla Conference, 90
Sixth Dalai Lama, 43, 47-49 49
Social structure, 73, 75, 77, 78
Sonam Topgye, 51
Songtsen Gampo, 16-18, 59
Switzerland, 116, 117

Tantricism, 29, 32
Tax system, 12, 61, 69, 76, 77
Tengyur, 67
Thirteenth Dalai Lama, 39, 89-92
Thomas, Lowell and Lowell, Jr., 2-3
Trade, 11, 55, 77
Treaties, 20, 55, 90, 106
'Tribute' missions (to China), 31, 32
Trisong Detsen, 19
Tsangpo (river), 9, 57, 74, 75, 113
Tsong Khapa, 32-33, 35
Tucci, Guiseppi, 46
Tu-fan, 11, 17

United Nations, 105
United States and Tibet, 97, 99, 101
Uprisings, 51, 107-108, 111, 114

Visitors, 2-3, 46-47, 91

Wheel of Life, 67
Women (status of), 79
World War II, 96-97

Yak, 10, 75

Yarlung, 9, 18
'Yellow Hats': *See* Gelupka
    (sect)
Yoga, 87
Younghusband, Col. Francis,
    54

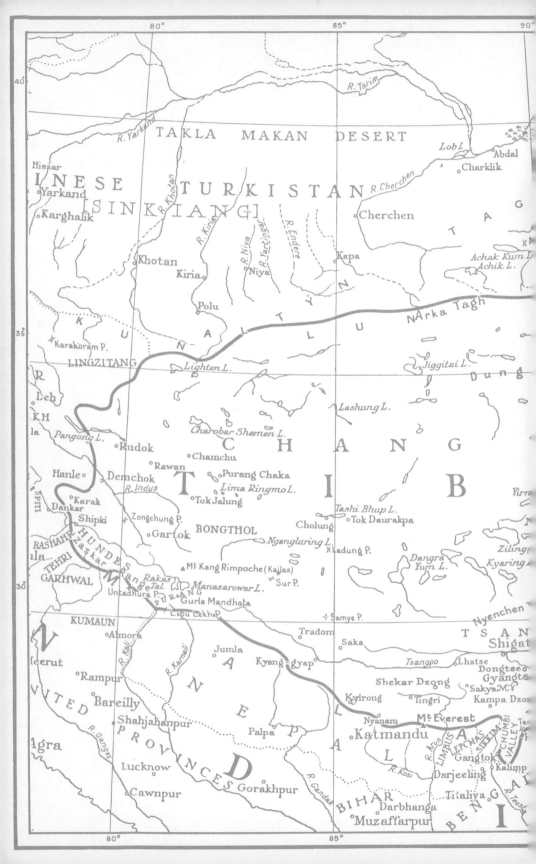